Erin McGoff is an award-winning filmmaker and content creator – known as the 'internet's big sister' through her AdviceWithErin branding. McGoff has built a significant online presence with millions of followers, delivering candid career and life advice for Gen Z and Millennials. She received a Pulitzer Fellowship in 2017 and was named a *Forbes* 30 Under 30 recipient in 2025. Her impact has been recognized by publications like the *New York Times, Washington Post, Wall Street Journal, Business Insider* and others, and she is currently a contributor to *CNBC*. McGoff lives in Washington, DC, with an occasional trip up to her cabin in the Catskills she custom-built, with her husband, Michael, and dog Olive.

The Secret Language of Work

HYPER-HELPFUL SCRIPTS FOR EVERY SITUATION

Erin McGoff

MICHAEL JOSEPH

PENGUIN MICHAEL JOSEPH

UK | USA | Canada | Ireland | Australia
India | New Zealand | South Africa

Penguin Michael Joseph is part of the Penguin Random House group of companies whose addresses can be found at global.penguinrandomhouse.com

Penguin Random House UK,
One Embassy Gardens, 8 Viaduct Gardens, London SW11 7BW

penguin.co.uk

First published in the United States of America by Portfolio,
an imprint of Penguin Random House LLC 2026
First published in Great Britain by Penguin Michael Joseph 2026
001

Copyright © Erin McGoff, 2026

The moral right of the author has been asserted

Penguin Random House values and supports copyright. Copyright fuels creativity, encourages diverse voices, promotes freedom of expression and supports a vibrant culture. Thank you for purchasing an authorized edition of this book and for respecting intellectual property laws by not reproducing, scanning or distributing any part of it by any means without permission. You are supporting authors and enabling Penguin Random House to continue to publish books for everyone.
No part of this book may be used or reproduced in any manner for the purpose of training artificial intelligence technologies or systems. In accordance with Article 4(3) of the DSM Directive 2019/790, Penguin Random House expressly reserves this work from the text and data mining exception

Illustrations by Janis Ozolins
Book design by Nicole Laroche
Printed and bound in Great Britain by Clays Ltd, Elcograf S.p.A.

The authorized representative in the EEA is Penguin Random House Ireland,
Morrison Chambers, 32 Nassau Street, Dublin D02 YH68

A CIP catalogue record for this book is available from the British Library

HARDBACK ISBN: 978-0-241-80254-0
TRADE PAPERBACK ISBN: 978-0-241-80255-7

Penguin Random House is committed to a sustainable future
for our business, our readers and our planet. This book is made
from Forest Stewardship Council® certified paper.

To Michael, my husband.

And to Chris and Claire, my parents.

Contents

INTRODUCTION — ix

CHAPTER 1
Change Your Words, Change Your Life — 1

CHAPTER 2
Small Tweaks, Huge Difference — 17

CHAPTER 3
The Art of Written Communication — 54

CHAPTER 4
Network Without Cringing — 69

CHAPTER 5
The Hidden Etiquette of Interviews — 99

CHAPTER 6
Negotiate Without Being Awkward — 135

CHAPTER 7
How to Set Boundaries and Expectations — 162

CHAPTER 8
How to Advocate for Yourself Without Being a Jerk — 183

CHAPTER 9
How to Deal with Sticky Situations   196

CHAPTER 10
How to Quit Your Job Gracefully   226

CONCLUSION
Words Are Powerful   241

ACKNOWLEDGEMENTS   245
NOTES   249
INDEX   251

INTRODUCTION

Most play checkers, few play chess.

Let me tell you a story about Samantha and Jessie. Samantha and Jessie have a lot in common. They're both nineteen. They have the same major at the same university. They're both applying for the same internship at the same consulting firm. And today is the first time either of them will be sitting down in a formal, corporate interview setting.

Samantha grew up in an upper-class family in a wealthy suburban neighbourhood. You know, the kind of neighbourhood with a Homeowners Association, Christmas carolling and a members-only golf course. Her dad's a CEO and her mum's an attorney. Samantha grew up attending private school, taking French lessons and 'summering' in Martha's Vineyard. You get the picture.

Jessie, on the other hand, grew up in a more rural blue-collar town. Her father is a truck driver and her mum works at a petrol station, and every month it's a challenge for them to make ends meet. Jessie's parents taught her how to work hard, be honest and have integrity. They always wanted her to have more opportunities than they did, but as a kid she didn't have access to much living in their small town. She spent her summers babysitting her little siblings, reading books from the library, and cooking with her grandma. She's the first person in her family to go to college.

Flip back to the present day where Samantha is sitting in the lobby of Health Inc., a corporate consulting firm. She gets called in, walks into a conference room and sits down with proper posture – her hands gently folded in her lap, both feet firm on the floor and a friendly smile on her face as she leans slightly forward. When the recruiter walks in, Samantha stands up, smiles, and gives a firm handshake partnered with a 'Hi Kelly, I'm Samantha, nice to meet you.' In her mind, she can hear her mum saying, 'You want to show them, not tell them – speak with your body.'

The recruiter asks Samantha, 'So, why should we hire you?' Samantha recalls her father's advice, reminding her to 'make it about the company, not yourself. Speak to your skills, and speak slowly.'

'I believe I am a great fit for this role for a few reasons,' Samantha answers. 'First, I'm a dedicated student with a three point nine GPA. I show up on time, am enthusiastic, and am a team player. Second, I'm particularly interested in public health consulting and genuinely fascinated by the vaccine research Health Inc. is conducting. I'd be honoured to contribute to future publications in any capacity. And finally, my experience volunteering with local organizations and my research-related coursework means I'd be bringing more to this role than a typical intern. If hired, I'd bring research skills, genuine curiosity, and an eagerness to learn and contribute.'

Next up, there's Jessie. She walks into the corporate lobby thirty minutes too early feeling nervous and a bit out of place in her brand-new suit. It's her first time wearing a suit. Is she supposed to button the jacket? What about her backpack? Can she leave it with the receptionist? Jessie awkwardly stands in the corner of the lobby avoiding eye contact and glued to her phone. When she gets called in for the interview, she shoves her phone into her backpack and spits out a string of apologies. After scurrying into the office, she plops down into her chair, bounces her leg and gives a timid and quick handshake to the recruiter after they initiate.

When the recruiter asks, 'So, why should we hire you?' Jessie fumbles a bit. She isn't sure why the recruiter is asking such a blanket question – it seems obvious. She thinks, *Don't you need an intern . . . ?*

'Uh, well, you should hire me because – wait – this is just an internship, though, right? So you're not really *hiring* me, it's just for the summer,' she says. 'But anyway, you should pick me because, well, I'm in school for business, and we had this guest speaker come in, and well, I'm interested in learning more about it all. To be honest, I'm not sure how the world of consulting works, but I'm definitely interested in gaining experience for my résumé. Oh, I'm also a hard worker and always show up on time! So . . . yeah. That's it I guess.' Jessie smiles and checks the recruiter's face for feedback. They move on to the next question.

After the interviews conclude, the recruiter emails her manager: 'I think we should go with Samantha. She seemed more interested. Let's invite her back for another interview.'

Samantha goes on to get the internship while Jessie gets the classic do-not-reply auto-rejection email. After graduation, Samantha goes on to accept a full-time position at the company and negotiates her salary, boosting her entry level pay by $4,000. Jessie accepts a job that underpays her, and she doesn't say anything because, well, negotiating would be rude and ungrateful, right?

The problem here isn't with Jessie or Samantha's ability, intelligence, motivation or drive. It's that one of them knows the secret language of work, a way of communicating that is used by successful, high-performing people to get what they want, while the other does not. And here is where we begin.

The Hidden Curriculum

Remember how in school you were taught that Tokyo is the capital of Japan and the mitochondrion is the powerhouse of the cell (but they somehow skipped over how taxes and mortgages work)? Those were part of the school curriculum, the visible curriculum. But remember how you also learned that you can't just sit wherever you want in the lunchroom? Like, the sixth graders sit near the bathrooms, the seventh graders sit near the teachers, and the eighth graders get the best spot – next to the windows? These are things you aren't explicitly taught but instead learn through observation. They are part of what's called the hidden curriculum: unspoken social rules of how to interact in a society.*

The secret language of work is part of the hidden curriculum. It's a set of unwritten rules and etiquette that communicates to others that you are professional, competent, experienced, dependable and trustworthy. These secret rules aren't written down anywhere, but rather embedded in our psychology and passed down in hushed tones through the networks of high achievers. Some folks will spend decades of trial and error simply attempting to pick up on tiny bits of this secret language, while most never learn of its existence. But you're in luck. In this book, I've compiled the unwritten rules of the secret language of work all in one place for you, so that you can reach your goals faster and with more confidence.

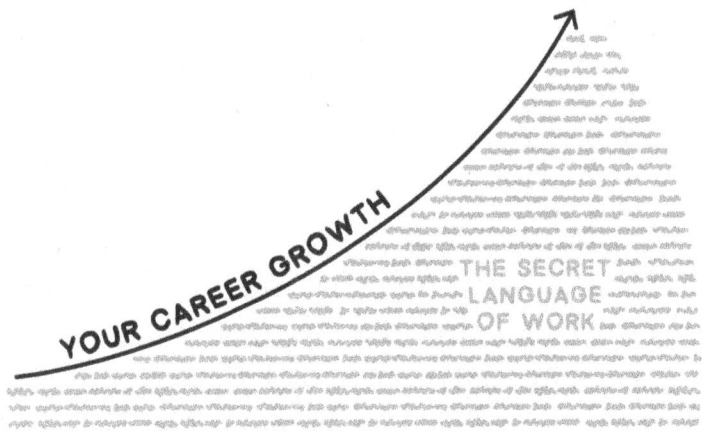

---

*Philip W. Jackson coined this phrase in his 1968 book *Life in Classrooms*, which explores implicit lessons, values and social norms that are learned in school but are not part of formal education.

My Story

So, why should you listen to me? Why should you spend hours of your precious time invested in yet another professional development book promising to change the way you approach your career (and life)? Allow me to introduce myself.

Hi, I'm Erin, also known as AdviceWithErin. Let's rewind a little. In 2020, when the pandemic hit, I was living in my four-hundred-square-foot Brooklyn apartment, confined by stay-at-home quarantine policies and living off my emergency fund. Before COVID-19, my career was going great. I had my dream job in the film industry, making good money, and gearing up to direct my second feature film. I had moved to New York at twenty-three, fresh on the heels of my Pulitzer Center reporting fellowship and the premiere of my debut feature documentary film, *This Little Land of Mines*.

I always knew my dream was to work in the film industry, but I wasn't born with access to the Hollywood industrial machine. I didn't know a soul in LA or New York, so I had to wiggle in on my own. I scraped and clawed my way into the industry, trying my best to network, be a sponge and learn the lingo as quickly as possible. And now I had accomplished my goals and had exciting things lined up. I felt like I had made it – it was all happening! You know, until the world imploded.

As the work dried up and shoots were delayed, bored and sad pandemic Erin had a burgeoning curiosity that led her to download an exploding social media app all the cool kids were using. I was instantly fascinated by TikTok's powerful algorithm. You could have zero followers and post a video that would magically reach the right audience. I decided to post some career advice, specifically about the very gatekept film industry, in the hopes of helping other 'outsiders' like me break in. I expanded to posting about networking, interviewing, cold emailing and even personal finance tips as the videos started to reach audiences from all industries.

One day, I propped my phone up on my window A/C unit and decided to post a tutorial on 'How to answer the worst job interview question ever: Tell me about yourself.' I edited it, clicked post and went to bed. I woke up the next morning and checked my phone. That video had gone viral overnight and garnered over twenty million views. Over the next few weeks, I gained hundreds of thousands of followers, and my DMs were flooded with people wanting more. I realized there was a massive need for practical, candid and realistic career advice.

This is the part of the story where I tell you I hit my big break, right? I jumped into content creation with two feet, got an agent, started coaching, penned a book deal, did a TED Talk, was interviewed on *Good Morning America*, and started selling massively successful online courses. The only thing? Well ... that didn't *quite* happen.

Personally, I wasn't super interested in being an 'influencer', or 'internet person', as I lovingly call it. I had a 'real job' at National Geographic and was developing my next documentary project with a studio. In the mornings and evenings, I made TikToks, and my following kept growing. I'd take a topic, research it, and design a video that both educated and entertained. It was something I did for fun, as a silly creative outlet.

But the feedback I was receiving from followers was anything but silly. I received hundreds of messages, sometimes thousands per week, from folks telling me about how my advice impacted their lives. They were able to bump up their salaries, advocate for themselves in meetings, professionally articulate their feelings, negotiate promotions, boost their confidence, and on and on.

One day, I posted a video about how to write that you worked at McDonald's on your résumé. To viewers, it seemed funny and random, but I did it very intentionally. McDonald's is one of the largest employers in the United States, yet it is a job that many struggle to be proud of. So I thought if I could teach people how to articulate the fact that they didn't just 'take orders', but rather 'managed customer payments via a POS system fulfilling more than 1,500 orders per shift', I could help empower them. The video exploded. Again, I received messages from people all over the world telling me never to stop doing what I was doing, and how much these videos had changed their lives.

So, no, as of writing this book, I'm not a self-proclaimed guru, I don't have a PhD in organizational psychology (yet), a lucrative life coaching business and forty-plus years of HR experience.

That's not me. Instead, I'm more like your friend's successful cousin who corners you at her birthday party and tells you to quit your job because you're too amazing to be underpaid while putting up with your lame boss. And then I follow up the next day to give you the exact words and timeline to quit professionally, proceeding to hop on FaceTime to help you revise your résumé and land your dream job.

I've helped literally millions of people from all different backgrounds gain the ability to get what they want – whether that's a million-dollar net worth or simply a new job that doesn't make them cry in a toilet cubicle. My advice is backed by psychological research and real-life case studies and is relevant for the modern-day worker. I have a zeal for creating meaningful change, with a dangerous level of curiosity and a tragically open mind. I believe there is no one right way to do anything – anyone who tells you they have all the answers and everyone else is wrong is selling you something. I believe in shutting up and listening to many, many wise folks who have gone before me and distilling their advice down to what is repeated over and over because it works. By reading this book, you are gaining access to some of the best advice I have gathered from the world's greatest minds.

Of course, I also have personal experience both hiring and getting hired as a business owner and freelancer who has worked with more than twenty-five companies across all industries. I have seen various company cultures, hierarchical structures, good and bad leadership, innovative and archaic policies, and have used all the different types of cloud-based collaboration tools. (Shout-out to Slack, I love you.) I understand what it's like to have an awful boss, but I also understand what it's like to have an awful employee or coworker. I've been on all sides and give advice that acknowledges all parties involved.

If you want to rise up in the world and be successful in what you set out to do, this book is for you. Maybe you graduated during or shortly after the COVID-19 pandemic and most of your professional experience has been through a screen. Maybe you're an introvert who can't stomach the thought of attending a networking event. Maybe you are early on in your career and simply lack confidence. Or maybe your career is going great, and you're just looking to take your communication skills to the next level.

Everyone has a unique story, and no one was born with any knowledge of the hidden curriculum. No one was born knowing how to ask for a recommendation or negotiate their salary or professionally quit their job. Everything anyone knows they learned from someone else, through either direct teaching or observation. So let's talk about what we're going to learn.

First, we're going to focus on the basics: small tweaks you can apply to any conversation to supercharge your professional (and let's be honest, personal) communication. We'll also learn how to build true inner confidence and get your mindset right. I want you to be operating with a confident, calm, genuine and clear mind. This will allow your words to be understood exactly the way you intend them to be.

Next, we'll discuss how to communicate professionally and effectively in some of the most common workplace scenarios. We'll discuss how to network without being awkward, negotiate without being rude, and instantly impress any recruiter without coming off as a try-hard.

Finally, we will dive right into all those sticky situations that no one prepares you for (and that you don't learn about in school). Situations like how to deal with an annoying coworker, give and receive feedback, quit a job you hate, ask for a raise (that your manager keeps saying is coming), and more.

But before we go any further, I'd like to point out something important – something that I didn't hear enough when I was rising up in my career. While I always recommend against spending any energy victimizing yourself, it is certainly worth acknowledging the fact that different people are viewed, well, differently in society. Therefore, what you say at work is going to be taken in a certain way based on how you show up in the world. No, this is not fair. And I'm not saying that you should mould yourself into someone you're not simply to change the way you're perceived.

My goal instead is to help you strike a balance between communicating professionally while still sounding like *you*. Feel free to take my advice and fit it into your personality. If you read one of my scripts and think, 'Oh my gosh, I would never say that,' then don't say it! Please do not say it. It will come off as disingenuous if you try to force it. You can still use the overall framework and change the exact words to fit your style.

As millions of people have asked me for advice over the years, I've noticed one thing over and over and over again. When people ask me for advice, they're really asking for two things: reassurance and validation. Their gut and heart already know what they want to do and what they want to say.

What holds people back from speaking up is fear. They don't want to ask for a promotion because they fear *rejection*. They don't want to negotiate their salary because they fear *failure*. They don't want to ask for a raise because they fear being *offensive*. They don't want to communicate burnout to their boss because they fear *embarrassment*. And they don't want to communicate their true thoughts to their team because they're afraid of making others *uncomfortable*.

Well, I have some good news: I'm here to teach you how to

communicate with confidence in a way that makes you and everyone around you feel good. That doesn't mean being a people pleaser; you can't always be the 'good guy'. Sometimes you need to give tough feedback, be straightforward, set a boundary, and break bad news. It's not your job to manage other people's emotions. It's your job to do your job.

However, there is a way to be a strong, effective and successful professional without being an unlikeable, selfish jerk. In fact, there is a way to assert yourself, take charge and speak confidently in a way that makes people like you more. This is the secret language of work, my friends. And get excited, because you're about to become fluent in it.

The Secret
Language
of Work

CHAPTER 1

Change Your Words, Change Your Life

Clear is kind. Unclear is unkind.

—BRENÉ BROWN

When I was a freshman in college, I landed an internship at a small commercial film production company. In my interview, I was eager to please. I said I could do anything! I'd stay late, work hard and do whatever needed to be done – even 'sweep the floors' if I had to. (Yes, I actually said that.) I pictured myself drafting call sheets, organizing the gear room, shaking hands with celebrities on set, reviewing scripts and learning from directors. I was so excited!

But the truth is, I had no idea what I was doing. I was merely a guppy out in the big blue sea, faking it until I made it. This was my first time working in a corporate environment, and I didn't know what to expect or what would be expected of me. What should I wear? Should I get to work early? How could I impress everyone around me?

To my dismay, I showed up on my first day (overdressed and

too early) and was introduced to my first task by an unenthusiastic post-production manager. 'You need to organize these files. It's pretty self-explanatory,' he said and left me alone in a dark, windowless room. It was just me, Excel, a hard drive and a broken dream.

I looked at the screen and saw files – lots and lots of files. I had to cross-reference them with a spreadsheet. It was menial, tedious, boring and unglamorous. (I mean, there were no celebrities!)

I quickly grew bitter. This was an unpaid internship. I was giving up three half days a week – days I could have spent working at a paid job – to do some random tasks alone in a room while learning nothing about filmmaking. I wondered if this was even legal.

But . . . I had told them I'd do anything, right? I couldn't blame them . . . right? In my interview, I had basically promised to do just this. I decided that as a rookie intern, I just had to bite my tongue.

Another producer who worked at the production company checked in on me every now and then (probably for proof of life). She was so nice, and I was hoping that one day she'd come to my rescue. But when she asked me how everything was going, I responded, 'Great!' I didn't know how to say in a professional way, 'I'm so bored I want to rip out my hair. Is there literally anything else I could do?'

Meanwhile, the aforementioned unenthusiastic post-production manager was often nowhere to be found. (I guess he was my boss? It was never clear.) When he did show his face, I'd remind him of my existence and ask him to check my work. I waited eagerly, daydreaming of him snapping out of it and saying, 'You're still doing this? I have a commercial that needs editing. How about you take over as our lead editor?' But alas, he never did.

It continued on like this for an entire semester. I eventually realized that I could get my work done pretty efficiently and spend the rest of the time watching Vimeo Staff Picks, eating Chinese takeout and doing homework. But overall, the internship was a bust. I learned very little and met almost no one.

It took me years to realize that to a great extent this was my fault. See, I never vocalized ... well ... anything. I wanted to be happy-go-lucky and help out wherever I could. I didn't want to offend anyone by complaining about the work I was being assigned. And I assumed that if I did a good job at my tasks, the people around me would notice and eventually give me more interesting things to work on. That, my friends, was my first crucial mistake: assuming anything about anyone, anytime, anywhere.

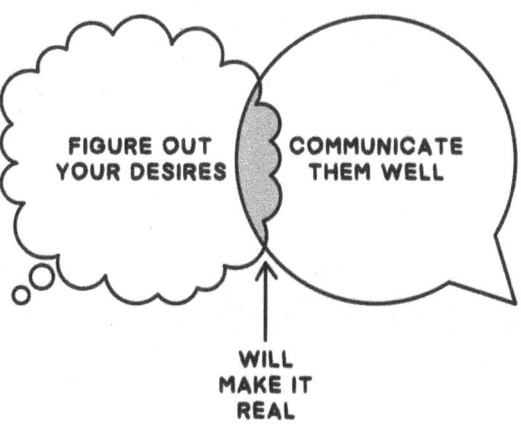

As my career progressed, I was able to observe and absorb the secret language of work – the language that highly successful people know how to speak to get what they want. I witnessed businesswomen smiling and even laughing as they negotiated deals. I saw colleagues smartly challenge each other on ideas and give blunt feedback that somehow wasn't offensive. I saw folks articulate their thoughts, share opinions, lead conversations and make tough decisions, all without any emotional baggage attached.

These people knew how to communicate professionally and perfectly curate their words to get across what they meant. They would never sit in a windowless room eating Chinese food for an entire semester. They would have looked at that room on day one and said, 'Yeah, this isn't going to work for me.' But, you know, in a professional way.

In fact, these folks probably wouldn't have been in that room in the first place because they would have asserted themselves in the interview. Maybe they would even have managed to negotiate for a stipend so that the internship wasn't completely unpaid. They knew how to professionally, effortlessly and joyfully advocate for themselves. I had so much to learn.

After that internship, I became obsessed with mastering the art of professional communication. How could I take my honest thoughts and turn them into effective, strategic communication? How could I be direct without being rude, confident without being cocky, assertive without being arrogant, and successful while still being liked? How could I learn this secret language that magically made everyone listen to and like me, all while still getting my way?

It took me a while, but through a *lot* of trial and error, I learned all this, and I went on to craft my dream career by using the secret language of work. After a few years of studying this hidden curriculum, I no longer had to blindly send résumés to apply for jobs or vent to my friends about annoying coworkers. I networked effectively and communicated proactively with decision-makers, and people were saying my name in rooms full of possibilities. As a result, the types of opportunities I dreamed of started finding me.

Maybe you're thinking, 'Good for you, Erin, but I'm an introvert and shy and just not outgoing and confident like you!' Well, I've got some news for you: I'm an introverted recovering people pleaser whose ideal Friday night is sitting on the couch under a heavy throw blanket watching a movie with my dog and husband.

In fact, many (dare I assume most?) successful people I know are actually quite introverted. Being an introvert, quiet or shy doesn't automatically mean you can't also be a powerful leader and have a wildly successful career. That's a narrative you have concocted for yourself, and I hate to say it, but it's not doing you any favours. Don't tell yourself a story that takes away your power. The only thing standing between you and what you want is you – no one else can give you what you want. It's up to you, my introverted little superstar. (Also, if you're an extrovert reading this, you're a superstar too.)

The Desired Outcome

Take a moment to picture yourself in the future, living your dream life. Not your parents', siblings' or friends' dream lives. Not my dream life. (I live on a ranch with a few dozen rescue dogs and own a bookshop café ... okay, snapping out of it.) Your dream life, whatever that looks like. I encourage you to dream, and to keep that dream close to your heart.

Remembering what you want is half the recipe for good communication. In Stephen Covey's book *The 7 Habits of Highly Effective People*, the second habit is: 'Start with the end in mind.' To plan the route to where you're going, you have to first *know where you are going*. What do you really want at the end of the day?

Moving forward, I will refer to this end result as your 'desired outcome', which is essential to keep in mind. Your desired outcome can be macro, like landing your dream job, or micro, like getting your boss to approve your holiday request. The important thing to know, though, is that once you are clear on your desired outcome, strategic communication is the key to getting it.

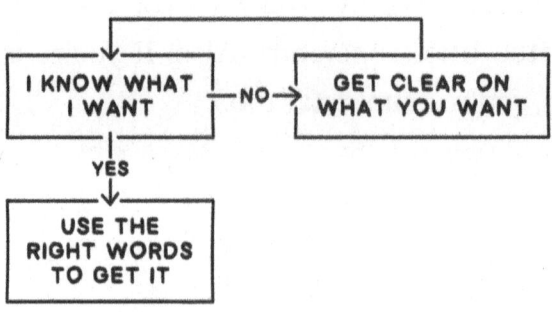

Most people treat talking as a means to an end – *I need to use mouth sounds to get what I want.* But words are incredibly powerful. Learning how to say the right words, in the right order, in the right way, at the right time is a rare skill that too few people invest in mastering. But those who do master it find that they quickly land on the fast track to achieving what they want. In fact, stellar communication is probably the most valuable career (and life) skill you can possess. Once you get the hang of it, you'll be shocked at how quickly and effortlessly amazing things start falling into your lap.

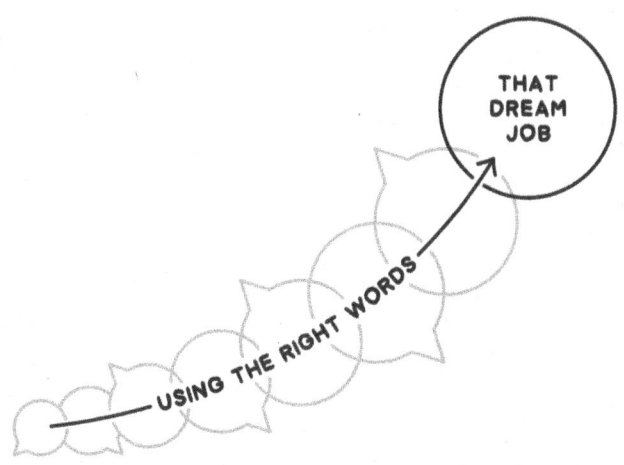

Remember the first line of this book? *Most play checkers, few play chess.* Checkers is a simple game that you play one move at a time. In the world of communication, this means that if someone makes you mad, you tell them they made you mad. Simple as that! But chess is about strategy, thinking several steps ahead, and remembering that every move you make needs to contribute to your desired outcome: winning the game. Good professional communication is chess. The obvious move isn't always the most advantageous for winning the overall game. You have to know how to play and think several steps ahead.

Workplace communication is about so much more than just making chitchat in the break room or figuring out what to say during those awkward 'We're just waiting on one more person to join . . .' first minutes of a Zoom call. No matter what kind of job you have or desire, communication is at the heart of every single aspect of your career. It is the key to getting a great job, a raise, a promotion, a mentor – the list goes on and on forever.

Sure, there are some other things you need to know in order to succeed at work. You need to be technically skilled for the job, dress appropriately, be on time and have a good work ethic. But in general, the difference between a competent worker with a very okay career and a competent worker with an incredible career is their ability to communicate effectively.

Every day I receive hundreds of messages, emails, and comments from my community asking for my advice on particular work challenges they're facing. And while at first glance these problems all seem completely different from one another other, nearly every single one of them boils down to the same issue: interpersonal communication. In fact, these people are all basically asking the same question: 'How do I tell [blank] [blank]?' For example:

'How do I tell my boss that I need a raise or I'm quitting?'
'How can I ask for an extra week of leave for my wedding?'
'How do I negotiate my salary when I have no experience?'
'How can I tell my coworker to stop using my mug?'

Here's something I need you to understand: Until AI takes

over completely and robots eradicate the human race, your boss will be a person, your company will be run by people, and your colleagues and clients will also be people. Professional communication is about dealing with other people. It's about relationships. And the only way to work well with people and get them to listen to and be open to your ideas and requests is to learn how to professionally communicate as a human to other humans. (Again, until AI takes over, and robots enter the chat.)

The Case for Professional Communication

If you can feel yourself bristling at the idea of professional communication in general and thinking, 'Ugh, I don't want to speak like those aforementioned robots,' I get it. A lot of people have a problem with the whole idea of trying to sound professional. They feel that professional communication signals and perpetuates classism and elitism. And just as I shared via Jessie and Samantha's story, there is absolutely some truth to that.

Yes, professional communication can feel unnecessary and time-consuming, I mean, just say what you mean, right? I used to think that way too, until I learned about the secret language of work and how powerful it can be. Imagine this: You're six months into dating someone you're really into, and they invite you to come meet their parents. You show up to their front door in your sweats with empty hands. You waltz inside, plop down on the couch, and say, 'So, Barb, what's for dinner?' You wouldn't do that, would you? (Please say no.) Even though that may be perfectly acceptable behaviour when rolling up to your best friend's house, it's not so appropriate in this scenario.

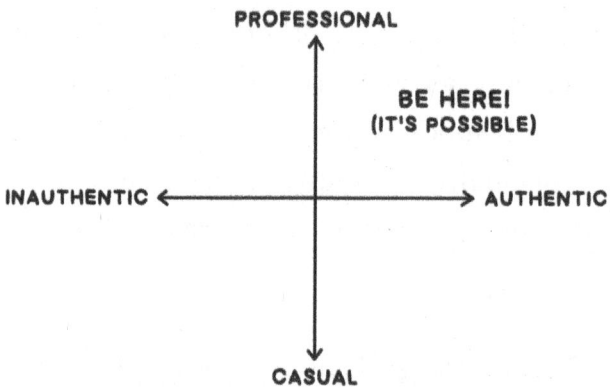

My point is that we all take on different personas in different environments. When meeting your new boyfriend or girlfriend's parents for the first time, you're going to put on your 'meeting the parents for the first time' persona. You're going to be on your best behaviour, show up with a gift, compliment the food, help clean up and try to impress them. Why? Because that's what's in your best interest: having a good relationship with your potential future in-laws! Remember, it's all about the desired result – it's chess, not checkers.

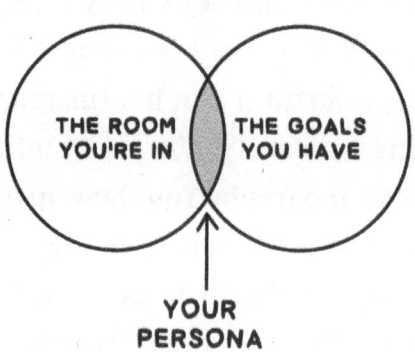

The same logic applies at work. It's important to have a work persona. It's not like you're being fake or pretending to be someone you're not. You're simply adjusting your behaviour to be your best self for the environment you're in. That way, you can more easily separate your professional life from your personal life. Don't try to bring your 'full self' to work, unless you want work to start expecting your 'full self'.

It took me a long time – years! – to learn these skills, partially because a lot of the existing advice on the subject didn't really speak to me. (Get it? Speak? I'll be here all week!) While I've read many excellent books and studies on professional communication, some of which I'll be referencing later on, I found that most advice encourages over-the-top professional speech, which can feel super phony and exclusionary. So, if all you've learned and been taught about professional communication before is to entirely change how you speak, dress, act and present yourself – I hear you.

We're all unique, and my problem with a lot of existing professional communication advice is that it made me feel like I had to put myself in a box and pretend to be someone I'm not. I had to turn off my sense of humour, tiptoe around what I mean, stop being too friendly, but also smile more? On one side of the spectrum, there are communication experts encouraging us to 'lead with your authentic self', or 'walk in your truth', but . . . what does that even mean? It's so squishy. Do I have to wear certain shoes to walk in my truth? How does this translate to telling my boss I'm burned out – I need the words!

And then on the other side of the spectrum, there's this sort of hypermasculine communication advice that encourages us to be overly aggressive. Let's be real. I'm not going to stare down a twenty-four-year-old recruiter, ask for a $30,000 bump, and keep saying, 'No,' in a low voice until he gives me exactly what I want. That's just not me. He'd probably be weirded out and end up calling security. (And as I was being escorted out of the building, I'd be like, 'Fair enough.')

Don't get me wrong – tips like these are amazing for some people, especially if you're pitching or selling to a tough crowd, as I have done many times as a filmmaker. But they aren't always appropriate for everyone in every situation.

For example, picture a twentysomething who's straight out of college trying to negotiate a sales commission upon a job offer. They could definitely try to apply masterful negotiation tactics and play hardball, treating the conversation like the art of war. But they'd probably be viewed as naive, overconfident and stubborn. If you communicate in a way that isn't genuine, people notice.

Or take me. I'm a five-foot-tall blonde girl who generally likes to smile a lot and is a recovering people pleaser. This type of aggressive communication would make me feel like I'm acting as 'Tough guy #1' in a police drama or playing a level 10 game of mental *Tetris*. The bottom line? No one is going to feel confident when they're communicating in a way that feels inauthentic to who they are as a person. (Hey, maybe that's what they mean by 'Lead with your authentic self!')

Despite all this, I firmly believe there is a good reason to learn 'workspeak'. For one thing, it helps you maintain boundaries at work. Your colleagues aren't your besties, nor should they be! You may be friendly with those you work with, but your professional relationships should be different from your personal ones. Learning how to communicate in a professional manner will help you set firmer boundaries with your job, which in turn, benefits you.

The Case for Jargon (Yes, I Mean It!)

I do agree that 'workspeak' can go way too far, especially when it comes to jargon. All the circle-back-iterations-of-implementations-to-reach-core-milestones make me want to scream. Corporate jargon, industry buzzwords and passive expressions can make it nearly impossible to decipher what people actually mean.

For example, back when I was interviewing for my first internship, the interviewer arrived late and immediately apologized, explaining that they were running a fire drill. 'Oh,' I responded, 'I didn't hear an alarm.' He looked at me like I was crazy. 'It's just a figure of speech,' he explained.

To this day, I have no idea why he was late or what they were doing, but apparently there was no actual fire. He was using corporate jargon, a figure of speech, which is a part of the secret language of work, one that varies according to the industry. For example, if you work in consulting, you might hear all about 'core competencies' and 'synergy' and get confused about why anyone is planning to 'boil the ocean'. If you work in marketing you may hear a lot of three-letter acronyms like 'KPIs', 'CTAs', and 'CPCs' being tossed around the room like

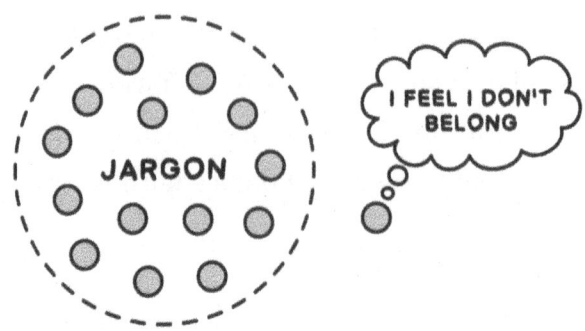

volleyballs. If you work for a nonprofit, you're probably going to hear a lot about 'impact', 'stakeholders' and making a 'soft ask'.

It can be fun to hate on jargon, and many people do, but it's still important to learn your industry's unique jargon so you can choose to 'talk the talk', so to speak, when necessary. There is so much annoying jargon in my industry, the film industry. (If I have to cut one more presales first look deal sizzle to provide proof of concept...) But I've made a point of learning it so I can communicate as effectively as possible.

Plus, jargon exists for a reason. It typically serves one of two purposes. For one, it can make things more efficient and basically act as a shortcut. This type of jargon usually comes in the form of acronyms: EOD (end of day), B2B (business to business), ROI (return on investment), POC (point of contact), etc. I mean, I think we can all agree that saying 'KPI' is much easier than saying 'key performance indicators' every single time.

And second, jargon can be used to soften the blow of a statement that might otherwise sound harsh (an excellent example of the secret language of work!). For example, phrases like 'Let's take this offline,' or 'Let's circle back,' are nicer ways of saying, *Read between the lines! You're wasting everyone's time, Steve, let's move on!* 'I was affected by restructuring' is a gentler way of saying, *Yeah, my company laid me off for no reason. Guess my job was no longer important.* And 'I'm currently at capacity but I'll let you know if some real estate opens' is a softer way of saying, *I am literally so stressed and overworked I cannot handle one more thing.*

You can choose to use jargon a lot or very little (if at all), but it's a language that you need to at least learn to understand so you have the choice. There is a massive difference between fluffy, corporate, robotic jargon and tactful, strategic communication. It's easy to be long-winded, use big words, and toss around next-gen industry jargon. You know what's not easy? Communicating simply. Simple is hard.

A great way to quickly learn your specific industry-related jargon is to listen to podcasts that are by and for people in your line of work. For example, if you're looking to get into real estate, browse Spotify, Apple podcasts, or whatever you use, to find real estate professionals who host consistent, up-to-date podcasts about the industry. Throw it on as you work out, cook or commute, and you'll slowly start to learn the lingo without even trying. This will help you grasp the nuance of what people at work are saying to you and help you avoid looking silly by asking, 'Oh, which wi-fi provider do you use?' when your co-worker tells you they have 'low bandwidth'.

And one more note about jargon? Don't use it with people who aren't in your industry. Telling your hometown friends about your job using niche, industry-specific jargon isn't impressing anyone, it just makes you look weird and pretentious. Only use jargon with folks you're sure also use that jargon. This is why I recommend against using jargon on résumés, unless it's an industry-wide, regularly used term. Use jargon where it's appropriate. Otherwise, you just look unprofessional.

REMEMBER, LANGUAGE IS POWERFUL. If you take some time to read the rest of this book, put my advice into practice, and get comfortable communicating at work, you will become an unstoppable force that everyone is obsessed with and who has the confidence to go after any dream you have. Let's start with the basics.

CHAPTER 2

Small Tweaks, Huge Difference

> Sometimes the most modest changes can bring about enormous effects.
>
> —MALCOLM GLADWELL

Meet Callie, a twenty-five-year-old outreach assistant at a university alumni office. She is a bright, competent hard worker who prides herself on being a fun, likeable personality in the office. But because she never learned the secret language of work, she frequently makes small rookie mistakes that inevitably hold her back from promotions and raises.

For example, Callie gets stressed out when people don't respond to her emails and sometimes writes back saying, 'Hellooooooooo?! :)).' And after being at her job for a year, she is feeling insecure and unsure about how to ask for a raise. She messages her boss, who is sitting in the next room, saying, 'hiii, I just found out I have to start paying my student loans next month so could I get a raise? any extra would help lol.'

Callie's boss appreciates the work she puts in, but is hesitant to promote her or have her interact with alumni or donors because her communication style is so... unpolished. In this case, it's not that Callie is making huge tactical errors, like I did at my first internship. She's just a little rough around the edges, which will perpetually hold her back without her even realizing it. She needs to make small tweaks to the way she communicates in order to rise up in her career.

Indeed, sometimes the smallest changes can make the biggest difference. Over time, they compound to make us feel and appear more professional, competent and powerful. That's what this chapter is all about: the small communication tweaks you can start implementing today that are the secret sauce that high performers use to supercharge their careers.

These small changes in the way you communicate fall into three main categories: mindset, the spoken word and body language.

Mindset: A Two-Part Guide to Confidence

To help you master the art of professional communication, I am going to spend the majority of this book giving you specific scripts – actual words to say in all different types of workplace scenarios that will help you get to your desired result. However, I beg you to heed my warning: Words alone, no matter how brilliant and savvy, will not sound right or be effective if you use them without the right mindset. So we need to spend a little bit of time first getting your head in the right place.

This professional communication mindset comes down to two main elements: self-awareness and confidence.

SELF-AWARENESS

In all areas of life, including work, self-awareness should be the goal. Why? When you are conscious of important things like what you want and why you want it, what you don't want and why you don't want it, why you find one coworker's voice so grating, why your boss has an uncanny way of getting under your skin, and so on, you become better able to set your emotions aside and calmly use the right words to navigate these situations.

We so often carry our past experiences, emotions and false narratives (the stories we tell ourselves about what's really going on – which are often exaggerated at best and fiction at worst) into our workplace communications. This can lead us to speak and act in ways that do not serve us. When you become aware of your emotions and false narratives and how your past is impacting your present, it becomes far easier to react objectively and stick to the script – literally – in order to get to your desired result.

Here's an example: Jenna has a coworker named Paul whose communication style is no-nonsense and a bit curt. This really bothers Jenna, and she finds herself getting upset anytime she's in a meeting with him. She checks in with her coworkers to see if they feel the same way, but no one seems to track with her. Some even like Paul's directness and don't find him annoying or rude at all. Jenna tries to get along with Paul, but sometimes she just can't help herself from lashing out or even accusing him of being mean. This causes a rift between them that makes working together really difficult.

Now, imagine that Jenna does the work to gain self-awareness around why Paul's communication style bothers her so much. Maybe she realizes that Paul isn't an especially mean person, but his mannerisms, the way he speaks, and even the way he looks subconsciously remind Jenna of her ex-boyfriend. When Paul's tone mirrors her ex, Jenna feels anger bubble up inside of her that ultimately has nothing to do with Paul.

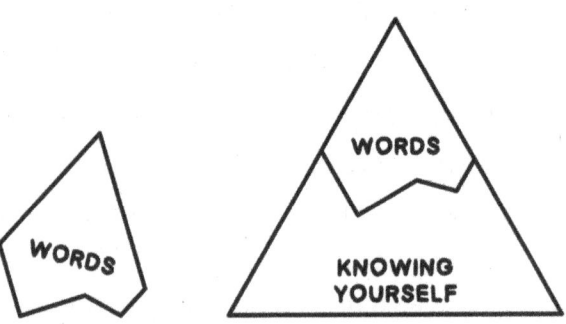

With this awareness, every time Jenna starts to feel that anger, she reminds herself, 'He's not my ex – he's just Paul from IT. He never cheated on me.' This helps her communicate calmly and professionally so she can develop a much better working relationship with Paul.

Everyone has certain communication styles that trigger their emotions. It will benefit you in many ways to take some time to work on understanding yourself in this way. Personally, I find myself getting frustrated when people take a long time to get their point across. But this is something I know about myself, and I realize it is 100 per cent the result of growing up in a big family on the East Coast. (If you know you know – gotta talk fast!) So if I'm in a meeting with a slow talker, I remind myself that's it's perfectly fine and I need to exercise patience instead of letting my frustration get in the way of our working relationship.

CONFIDENCE

First of all, I want you to know that it is completely normal to not feel super confident early on in your career. You have a lot to learn, and it would be weird if you had 100 per cent bulletproof confidence on day one. Humility is a virtue.

However, confidence is absolutely essential if you want to master the art of professional communication. Saying the right words is one thing. Saying them from a place of confidence is another.

The good news is that as you advance in your career and gain more experience, you will naturally become more confident. Plus, simply knowing that you have the right words in your back pocket to say in any situation that presents itself at work will help you feel more confident too.

But first, wait, what even is confidence, really? Confidence is not about trying to get everyone to like you. That's ego. When you are truly confident, you acknowledge your mistakes and work on your flaws, but at the end of the day, you don't really care if others like you or not, because you genuinely like yourself and are proud of who you are – and your opinion of yourself is most important. Real confidence doesn't come from external validation like awards, followers, money or attention. It comes from the inside and the view you have of yourself. This is something that no one can give you or take away from you.

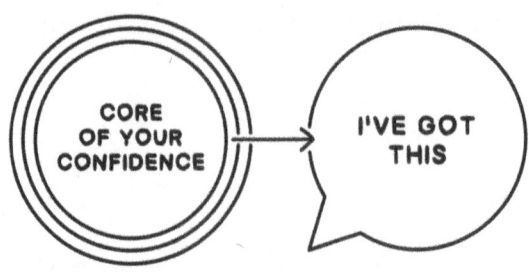

There will be days when you feel more or less confident than others, and that's okay. Confidence isn't binary – it's a spectrum. Working on building your confidence simply raises the threshold. Think of your confidence as a houseplant. It's there, thriving in the sun, but it needs regular watering to stay alive. To water your confidence, keep honing your skills so that you witness yourself improving, surround yourself with people who champion you, and keep the promises you make to yourself.

But the real key to confidence is being your own best friend. We all have a voice inside our heads that is yapping 24/7. For most of us, this voice is often extremely mean, judgemental, paranoid and critical. It tells you that you're not good enough, you're not worthy, you have no friends, you'll never succeed, you're doing everything wrong, and on and on.

If you let this voice keep going like this without ever calling it out, you will never achieve true confidence. No one spends more time with you than you, so the way you talk to yourself matters!

Starting today, work on noticing that voice inside your head. The next time it says something negative, I want you to respond the way you would if a best friend was saying this about herself. For example, if you make a mistake at work and that voice mutters, 'You're so dumb, and all your coworkers hate you,' pretend you just heard your best friend saying about herself, 'I'm so dumb, and all my coworkers hate me.' How would you respond?

Would you say, 'Yeah, that's true, you're so dumb and all your coworkers hate you'? No! (At least, I hope not!) You'd say, 'Oh, shut up – you're not dumb. Your coworkers don't hate you. Some of them might be annoyed at you for missing that deadline, so don't miss the next one. You're doing great. Stop being so hard on yourself!'

Notice how a true BFF doesn't sugarcoat it with a heavy layer of toxic positivity, but instead is encouraging while giving it to you straight. This is how I want you to start speaking to yourself. Be your own ally, role model and best friend, and your confidence and success will start to soar.

The Spoken Word: Five Tiny Tweaks with Big Impact

Now that you're developing the right mindset, let's cover some small changes you can make to the way you speak that will help you get to your desired outcome. Many of the following tips boil down to one thing: becoming more articulate. This doesn't mean that you have to use big, fancy words or sound like you're living in eighteenth-century England. You can be articulate and still sound like you. Here are some of my favourite tips for becoming more articulate.

1. LISTEN TO ARTICULATE PEOPLE

We tend to subconsciously start to mimic the way the people around us speak. This is human nature. If all the people you hang out with are like, 'No cap I'm entering my funemployed era, I love that for me,' you're going to gradually start speaking this way, even if you don't mean to. So to become more articulate, try to surround yourself with articulate people.

If you're thinking, 'But, Erin, I live in a small town, and I'm sorry, but I don't have access to a posh country club of well-read gentlemen,' I get it, and I have an easy solution: the internet. Go to Spotify and listen to podcasts. Download Audible and listen to audiobooks. Go to YouTube and watch some TED Talks. Simply having articulate speakers in your ears will help you gradually upgrade your speech, without you even noticing. You'll discover new words and new phrases, and voilà – you are now a more articulate speaker.

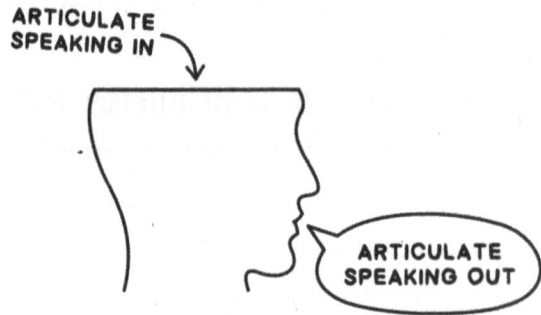

2. RECORD YOURSELF

It might be painful, but use your phone to record yourself talking about something, anything, for about five minutes. Then watch it back in three different ways. First, turn the audio off and just look at your body language. What are your hands, eyes, legs and face doing? (More on this in a moment.) Second, listen to the audio only, paying attention to where you stumble, mumble or overuse fillers. Finally, watch and listen at the same time. What do you notice? You might need to speak more slowly, cut down on 'ums', or stop twirling your hair (guilty). Then, record yourself all over again using any insights you've gained. If you keep doing this, improvements are inevitable.

3. SANDWICH YOUR THOUGHTS

Remember in high school when you learned how to write an essay and you had to include an introduction, three body paragraphs, and a conclusion? Think about speaking in a similar way, albeit without whole paragraphs. No one has time for that.

Basically, I'm asking you to sandwich your thoughts: Before asserting your opinion, acknowledge what was said beforehand. When wrapping up your opinion, acknowledge what may be said next.

For example, say you're in a meeting with a few colleagues deciding which way to go with a certain campaign. Your co-worker Rachel says, 'I like direction number two.' Internally, you disagree. But instead of jumping right in with, 'Direction three is way better,' take a moment to set the stage. Try, 'I also like number two, Rachel. However, direction three feels more in line with the campaign goals. What do you think?'

This 'sandwich' technique is also helpful when answering questions. You can repeat or rephrase the question as a lead-up to your answer. For example, say that in your annual review your boss asks you, 'What do you feel were some of your biggest wins this year?' You could just say, 'Well, let's see, the new policy I implemented worked really well to increase efficiency.' That's not a bad answer. But you'll sound more articulate if you say, 'One of my biggest wins this year was the new policy I implemented. It increased efficiency by thirty per cent, and I'm really proud of that. Would you agree?'

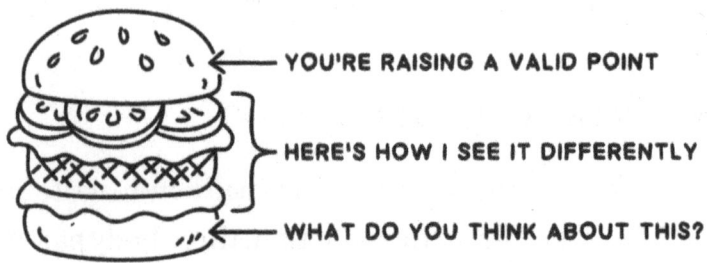

4. BE A GOOD LISTENER

This may sound weird, but one of the most effective ways to sound more articulate is by actually being a good listener. You may have heard of a little thing called 'active listening', which is about working to fully understand the meaning behind someone else's words.

The most important part of active listening (besides, you know, actually listening) is repeating back or paraphrasing what the other person said to make sure you fully understood them before you respond. This practice forces you to pay attention to and truly hear the other person instead of just waiting for them to stop talking so you can reply or project your own narrative onto their words.

Let's go back to the conversation with Rachel about which campaign to move forward with. Honestly, you are dead set on direction three. As the conversation continues, all you're thinking about is how you're going to convince her of your opinion. 'I really feel like direction two is best because it's sort of a callback to the Super Bowl ad that the brand did last year,' Rachel says. 'That continuity is really important.'

'Direction three is the way to go,' you pipe in as soon as she pauses. 'It's so exciting and fresh, and it will definitely capture viewers' attention.' Your opinion may be valid, but you sound sloppy delivering it, and Rachel is left feeling completely unheard, which only hurts your case. Plus, maybe she has a good point, but you totally missed it because you weren't really paying attention to what she was saying.

Now, imagine that you're practising active listening. Rachel says the same thing, but this time, you know that you're going to summarize her thoughts before offering your own, so you're listening attentively. When she finishes, you pause and think about what you want to say and how you want to say it. Rachel is really passionate about her opinion, so perhaps repeating it back will make her feel more heard, and in turn, more likely to listen to your arguments. You reply, 'What I'm hearing is that you believe having consistency in the messaging is the number one priority when choosing a campaign. Did I get that right?'

'Yes,' Rachel says, feeling grateful that she has been fully heard. 'I know you think direction three is more exciting, and I agree it's really cool, but for this particular brand, I think it's more important to be consistent than exciting. But my mind could be changed with a convincing argument!'

This time, no matter what decision ends up being made, Rachel knows that her option was truly considered. You have a more thoughtful, collaborative conversation, and you appear more considerate, attentive and articulate. Big win!

5. JUST. STOP. TALKING.

One of my greatest and most important pieces of communication advice? Stop talking! Talk is cheap, silence is golden, and sometimes the best response is no response. Treat each of your words like a gift you give away, and to quote Mahatma Gandhi, 'Speak only if it improves upon the silence.'

This includes embracing silence as soon as you're done making your point. You could make the smartest, most articulate statement on the planet and then ruin it when you end it by mumbling something like, 'So, yeah,' or 'Does that make sense?' or my personal favourite and one I use all the time, 'But anyway...' (I'm a work in progress too, y'all.)

This is a hard habit to break, but you'll sound so much more articulate when you just stop talking when you're done talking! If you're struggling to wrap up a statement or a presentation, swap out, 'So yeah, I guess that's it,' with something like, 'That's it from my end, and I look forward to hearing what you think,' or 'What questions do you have?' But make sure you end strong

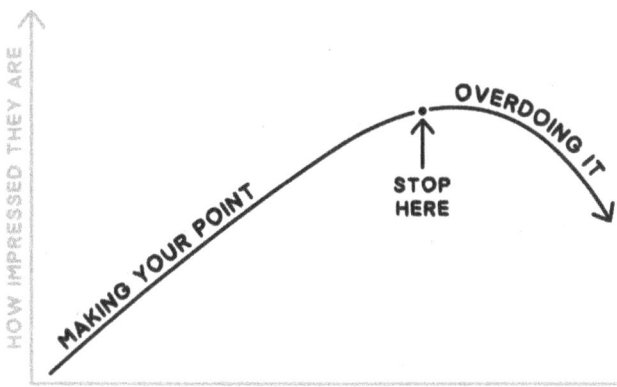

instead of trailing off! You know what I mean? Does that make sense? But anyway...

The Top Four Verbal Communication Fails

Now that you're working on becoming more articulate, let's cover some common communication pitfalls that are important to avoid. It's amazing how many of the problems we face at work really boil down to one (or more!) of the following:

1. MISTAKING ME PROBLEMS AND YOU PROBLEMS

Shelly is a twenty-nine-year-old remote worker at a large marketing firm, and her workload has recently become unmanageable. She is feeling burned out as she tries to keep up and stay in her boss's good graces. Week after week, Shelly keeps saying to herself, 'Next week it'll be easier,' but nothing changes. (Oh, the lies we tell ourselves.)

Time goes on, and Shelly is really struggling. Work is piling up, and she's getting it all done right and on time, delivering to her boss with a smile. But she is growing more and more resentful. Every time her boss Slacks her with a request, Shelly can feel her blood pressure rise. She doesn't know what to do about her overly demanding boss who has no respect for her time and energy.

What Shelly doesn't realize is that this is a 'Me Problem', meaning a problem with Shelly, not a 'You Problem', meaning a problem with her boss. See, Shelly has never told her boss that she is overwhelmed. Every time her boss asks her to do something, she says, 'You got it!' Shelly's boss has no idea that this workload is burning Shelly out.

Of course, you could argue that her boss should understand a proper workload – but that's a mindset that you need to quit. Thinking that others 'should' do this or that takes away your power and control. Some folks work incredibly efficiently while others need more time, and when you're managing multiple people, especially remotely, you don't have eyes on your team. You have to rely on honest, direct communication.

Because Shelly hasn't communicated to her boss about her workload, this is a Shelly problem (aka a Me Problem). If Shelly tells her boss that her workload is too heavy, then it would become her boss's problem (a You Problem).

Conflict often arises when people try to turn Me Problems into You Problems and expect others to solve problems that are not within their control. In Adlerian psychology, as laid out in the book *The Courage to Be Disliked* by Ichiro Kishimi and Fu-

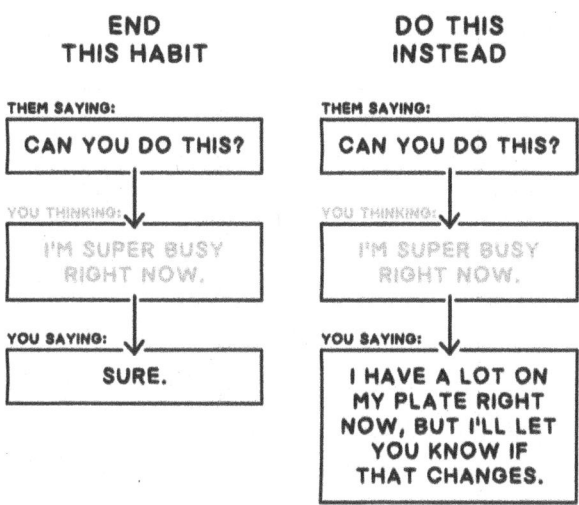

mitake Koga, this is referred to as 'a separation of tasks'. According to this theory, stress and imbalance in interpersonal relationships stem from people making their Life Tasks into your Life Tasks (aka their problems into your problems), or vice versa. You gain control over your life when you stop expecting other people to handle your problems for you and you stop trying to solve other people's problems for them.

Here's a more nuanced example to show the other side. One of my followers, Jen, sent me a message that in her one-on-one annual feedback session, her boss said that Jen was intimidating. She asked me for advice on how to come off as less intimidating. I asked her if this was feedback she received regularly, and if being intimidating had impeded her relationships before, and she said, 'No, this is the first time I've heard this!'

That told me that this wasn't a Me Problem for Jen. The problem wasn't that Jen was intimidating – it was that her boss was intimidated. That's a You Problem ('you' as in her boss).

Sure, Jen could decide to seek feedback from others to see if they felt similarly. If so, she could find ways to appear more approachable and friendly – like being warmer or making more of an effort during small talk. But Jen can't control how she's perceived by her boss. In this situation, all she can control is her communication with her boss and her actions thereafter. She may ask her boss, 'Thank you for your feedback. Are you able to share specific examples or recommendations on how I could be less intimidating moving forward?' But at the end of the day, it is Jen's boss and not Jen who needs to resolve this issue, as this is an issue of perception, not an objective action to be changed.

When a problem arises for you, ask yourself if it is actually a Me Problem. Do you have control over the outcome? If so, take responsibility and do what you can to work towards a solution. If you do not have control over the outcome, though, it's a You Problem (or a Them Problem, if you will). Don't take on other people's problems. Focus on addressing Me Problems instead, and watch your problems start to disappear!

Reflect: Think about a recent conflict at work. Would you categorize it as a Me Problem or a You Problem? Write down how you could address it using this framework.

2. NOT KNOWING WHAT KIND OF CONVERSATION YOU'RE HAVING

Now that you know the difference between Me Problems and You Problems, let's talk about the four categories of conversations. Two coworkers, Michael and Emily, are having a conversation in the break room about a project they're working on together that is offtrack. Emily is venting about how stressed she is. 'I couldn't sleep all night,' she tells Michael. 'I just kept thinking about how impossible it's going to be to meet this deadline.'

'There's a meditation app I use when I can't sleep,' Michael replies. 'Here, let me find the name of it.'

'No, forget it,' Emily says, growing frustrated. 'It's not about the sleep.'

'I'm just trying to help,' Michael says defensively.

'You can't help,' Emily says, 'unless you can go back in time and change the whole timeline of this project.'

'Then why are we even discussing it?' Michael says angrily.

'Honestly, I don't know!' With that, they both storm out of the break room.

What the heck happened here? Emily and Michael are trying to have two different conversations. Emily just wants to vent, and Michael is trying to offer solutions or information. This leaves Emily feeling unheard and Michael feeling frustrated.

Any time you speak to someone, you can have one of two types of conversations, factual or emotional, with two different goals, connection or change. A factual/connection conversation is about sharing information while strengthening relationships. A factual/change conversation is when you use facts to drive action or prompt change. An emotional/connection conversation is about sharing feelings to create empathy and strengthen bonds. And an emotional/change conversation is when you share emotions to drive reflection or suggest change.

The problem here is that Emily is trying to have an emotional/connection conversation, and Michael is trying to have a factual/change conversation. This disconnect is what is causing the conflict between them. Here are examples to show how each conversation type can serve different purposes:

1. **FACTUAL/CONNECTION**

    Scenario: Two coworkers are discussing the timeline of an upcoming project.

    - **Coworker 1:** 'The project deadline is tight, but that's pretty common for this type of client.'
    - **Coworker 2:** 'Yeah, I've noticed. It seems like we're always racing against the clock in this industry.'
    - **Goal:** They're exchanging information about the project (factual), but the conversation strengthens their bond (connection) as they acknowledge a shared understanding of the work environment.

2. **FACTUAL/CHANGE**

    Scenario: A manager is giving feedback to an employee on their performance.

    - **Manager:** 'I've noticed that the last few reports were submitted late. Can we work on getting those in by the deadline moving forward?'
    - **Employee:** 'I'll make sure to improve my time management and get the next one in on time.'
    - **Goal:** The manager is focusing on missed deadlines (factual) with the goal of prompting timely submission of reports (change).

3. EMOTIONAL/CONNECTION

Scenario: Two coworkers are talking about the stress of their workload.

- **Coworker 1:** 'This project is really starting to get to me. I feel like I'm constantly working and never catching up.'
- **Coworker 2:** 'I know what you mean. I've been feeling overwhelmed too. Want to go grab a coffee and talk?'
- **Goal:** The conversation is focused on sharing their stress (emotions), and the goal is to feel validated by expressing those feelings (connection).

4. EMOTIONAL/CHANGE

Scenario: A friend is offering advice to another who's feeling stuck in their career.

- **Friend 1:** 'I just feel so unmotivated at work lately. I'm not sure if this is the right path for me anymore.'
- **Friend 2:** 'I'm sorry you're feeling so down. Have you thought about looking for a new job or maybe talking to your boss about switching roles?'
- **Goal:** The first friend is expressing their lack of drive (emotional), and the second friend is using that emotional input to suggest exploring new job opportunities or roles (change).

With this in mind, let's go back to Michael and Emily. Let's say Michael has read this book (thanks, Michael!). Here's what he might do differently:

'I couldn't sleep all night,' Emily tells Michael. 'I just kept thinking about how impossible it's going to be to meet this deadline.'

'Yeah,' Michael agrees. He hears that Emily isn't communicating anything factual and is rather expressing her emotions. He knows this is an emotional conversation but needs to determine if the goal is connection (to be heard) or change (to be helped).

'I have some ideas,' he says, 'but right now do you want to be heard or helped?'

'Oh, just heard, I guess,' Emily says. 'I know there's nothing we can do to change it right now. It's just so unfair that they keep sticking us with these unrealistic timelines.'

'Totally,' Michael says. 'It's like they have no concept of how much work goes into this stuff.'

Emily nods. 'Well, I better get to it,' she says.

'Me, too,' says Michael. 'Let's check in with each other later and see how we're doing.'

'Sounds good!' Emily smiles, feeling better now that she got this off her chest.

Ta-da!

In addition to asking the other person if they want to be heard or helped, it's important for you to know what kind of conversation you want to have. Remember, desired outcome, people! Are you looking to share the results of the latest customer survey? That's a factual conversation. Do you just want to vent and be heard? That's an emotional conversation.

Knowing what type of conversation you want to have before addressing someone will help you get to your desired outcome.

Say you're going to tell your toxic boss that you're quitting your job. It may be tempting to tell him what a horrible person he is, but you know that your aim is to have a factual conversation. So stick to the facts and save the emotional conversation for happy hour with friends. Or therapy. Or both!

Reflect: Think about the last time a conversation at work went south. What type of conversation were you trying to have? Do you think the other person was trying to have a different type of conversation? What would have happened differently if you had aligned these expectations?

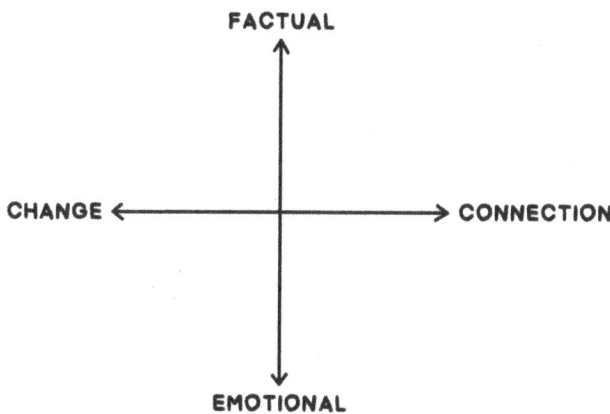

3. USING THE WRONG COMMUNICATION STYLE

Just like there are four types of conversations, there are four styles of communication: passive, passive-aggressive, aggressive and assertive.

First, let's start with passive communication. (Hello, fellow conflict-avoidant people pleasers, gather around!) Passive communication is when someone avoids expressing themselves entirely, aiming to avoid conflict at all costs. An example of this is your boss asking you if you can take on a new project when you're already completely overwhelmed with work, and you answer, 'Sure,' in an effort to please your boss and avoid conflict.

Second, passive-aggressive communication is when someone expresses themselves indirectly. They appear passive, but they show their emotion in subtle or indirect ways. Context here matters. If you take these comments out of context and look at them on paper, they probably wouldn't seem aggressive at all. For example, your boss schedules a meeting and says, 'Did you check your calendar to make sure you're not on vacation?' This doesn't seem aggressive at face value. But if your boss has commented several times that you've been taking too much leave lately, that context makes this question passive-aggressive.

Third, aggressive communication is when someone expresses themselves with no concern for how it might impact the other person, speaking solely from an emotional perspective. For example, if your boss says, 'Can you take on this new project?' and you respond, 'Are you kidding me!? Look at how much work I already have! And you want to give me more? This is ridiculous,' that is aggressive communication.

Finally, assertive communication is when someone expresses themselves in a strategic manner – prioritizing their desired outcome over their emotions. You probably don't need me to tell you that 99 per cent of the time, assertive communication is the way to go. This is true both in and out of the workplace, and the scripts throughout this book are focused mainly on quality assertive communication.

Before you speak, always ask yourself, 'Am I being assertive? Or am I being passive, passive-aggressive, or aggressive?' Training yourself to default to assertive communication doesn't just happen overnight. It's a muscle that you actively have to exercise. My passive friends – I need you to know that no one is mad at you, and, in the words of Brené Brown, 'Clear is kind.' Don't be afraid to be kind and clear. And to my aggressive friends, I need you to know that people can't hear what you're saying when they feel defensive. It's like they go on mute. Manage your emotions so they don't manage you. Strive to be assertive, kind, and honest in all that you say.

To give you a better idea, here are some examples of how to say basically the same thing in each of the four different styles:

Situation: Your coworker overpromised to a client and is now riding you to get something done in an unrealistic time frame. Your coworker comes up to your desk and says, 'Just checking in. What's the update? We need this to go to the client ASAP.'

Passive: I'm working on it . . .

Passive-aggressive: It's funny, usually project managers actually manage the clients . . .

Aggressive: Ugh, well, if you didn't tell the client that we could get this done today, then none of us would be in this situation!

Assertive: I'm concerned about the timeline here. To get this done properly, we need to push back on the delivery or the scope.

Situation: You and your colleague April each shared an idea in a meeting, and the team decided to go with April's idea. Again. You feel that the team favours her ideas because she's more outgoing and likeable.

Passive: Sure, let's just go with April's idea . . .
Passive-aggressive: April's ideas are just always better than mine, I guess.
Aggressive: It's not fair that everyone is just ignoring my idea and picking April's! This happens literally every single time!
Assertive: Hold on, I'd like to revisit my concept. I think it's really strong. Can I take you guys through it again?

Reflect: Think about the last time you were passive, passive-aggressive, or straight-up aggressive with someone at work. How could you have reframed your point in a more assertive manner?

4. UNDERUSING OR OVERUSING SOFTENERS AND FILLERS

Lastly, a 'fail' that I see a lot is the over- and/or underuse of softeners (like 'sorry') and fillers (such as 'just' or 'like'). When overused or not used strategically, these words can make you seem unprofessional. But I believe they do have a purpose, so it's important not to underuse them, either.

For example, let's say you have a strong personality and have received feedback that you come off as abrupt. One day, you need to break bad news to someone. Sure, you could say, 'Rick's not coming.' Or you could try saying, 'Sorry, Rick's not coming anymore.' Even though Rick not coming isn't your fault and you technically have nothing to apologize for, the use of 'sorry' here as a softener to balance out your strong personality is an effective communication strategy. If you don't want to say 'sorry', you can always try, 'Did you hear? Rick's not coming anymore,' or 'Oh, Rick's not coming.'

On the contrary, if you have a naturally softer personality, it might be wise to start cutting down on your 'sorrys'. For example, let's say your colleague made a typo in a presentation and the client wants it fixed. You don't have to say, 'Sorry, but would you mind fixing this typo, please?' You can just say, 'Hey, can you please fix this typo? Thanks.' This is exactly why it's so important to be aware of how you're perceived and gain self-awareness.

Likewise, filler words are normal, and speaking without using any of them can sound robotic, patronizing and downright weird. You end up sounding like a pastor or a news anchor. It's just not natural. It's the overuse of fillers that, like, causes, um, problems. You know?

That said, one tip I love is to use higher-quality fillers to sound more professional. If you overuse the word 'like', try replacing it with, 'for example'. Replace 'but' with 'however'. Be intentional with your fillers, and with time it will start to feel natural. Don't be afraid to experiment with language. That's how you'll find your style of sounding genuinely professional and authentic.

Reflect: Record yourself talking about a random subject for

five to ten minutes. Go back and analyze your speech to see filler words you tend to favour. Use this self-awareness to make adjustments moving forward.

Say This, Not That

Sometimes, better professional communication comes down to simple swaps – exchanging one word or phrase for another. In this section, I'll break down five common techniques successful people use every day as part of the secret language of work. Let's start with one of my favourites:

REPLACE 'WHY' WITH 'WHAT' OR 'HOW'

Imagine that your colleague Greg is editing a video with a program you've never seen before, and you genuinely want to understand what the heck he's doing. You ask him, 'Why are you doing it that way?' To Greg, this might sound a little judgy, like you're questioning his competence and decision-making. He gets defensive and says, 'Why don't you just let me do my job and you focus on writing the script for the next video like you're supposed to?' Yikes.

Now, imagine that instead you ask Greg, 'What technique are you using?' This shows curiosity instead of judgement, which makes Greg more likely to share his approach. 'Oh, I recently learned this new method that I'm finding way more efficient. Here, let me show you.'

One simple swap, and a totally different outcome. Think

about how this change might play out in all different workplace scenarios.

For example:

'Why did you move the meeting?' becomes 'What was the reason for moving the meeting?'

'Why do you think launching a week earlier would be a good idea?' becomes 'How do you think launching a week earlier would benefit the campaign?'

'Why did you assume it wouldn't work?' becomes 'How did you come to that conclusion?'

REPLACE 'BUT' WITH 'AND'

When we use the word 'but', it tends to negate everything we said before it, even if we don't mean it to. If you don't believe me, think about this in an out-of-work context. How would you feel if someone said to you, 'I love you, but you're kind of annoying'? That 'I love you' didn't count for much, did it?

The same thing goes for work, so be mindful of where you're placing your buts! Replacing 'but' with 'and' strikes a more collaborative and professional tone. If two things are true, use 'and' instead of 'but'.

For example:

'I can see that you've been working hard this year, but there are a few areas where I'd like to see improvement' becomes 'I can see that you've been working hard this year, and there are a few areas where I'd like to see improvement.'

'I've really been enjoying my work with the team, but I'd love to talk about adjusting my compensation' becomes 'I've really been enjoying my work with the team, and I'd love to talk about adjusting my compensation.'

REPLACE CLOSED-ENDED QUESTIONS WITH OPEN-ENDED QUESTIONS

Closed questions basically only allow for one of two answers: yes or no. These are binary questions like 'Do you like ice cream?' Not only are these questions conversation killers, they're also just boring and leave little opportunity for connection.

Instead, it's better to ask 'What kind of ice cream do you like?' or 'What's your favourite dessert?' These are open-ended questions, where the other party is prompted to elaborate. (For the record, if someone asks me if I like ice cream, my answer is yes. If they ask me, 'What kind of ice cream do you like?' my answer is also yes. All of the above. I don't discriminate. But also, Ben & Jerry's Half Baked – don't @ me.)

Here's a simple example: Imagine that you're working with a team to decide when to launch a new product for your company. You could ask, 'Should we launch this right after the new year?' In this case, no one is being encouraged to think through all the options, and it'll probably come back to you to do all the mental work. Maybe it makes more sense to launch this particular product earlier, in time for the holidays, or punt it to the spring, in time for spring break. Asking 'When do you think it would be best to launch this product?' would lead the team to explore the timing more broadly, possibly leading to a more successful outcome.

Here are a few more examples:

'Do you think we should add this new feature or not?' becomes 'How do you think this feature would improve this product?'

'Should I prioritize this project this week?' becomes 'Which tasks should I prioritize this week?'

'Is the client happy with the results?' becomes 'What was the client happy with, and were there areas where they felt there could be improvements?'

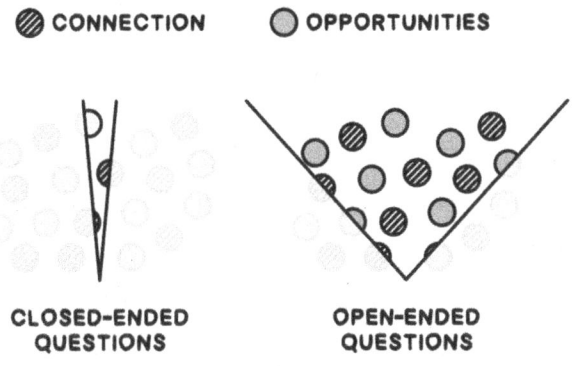

REPLACE NEGATIVE LANGUAGE WITH POSITIVE LANGUAGE

This goes back to my number one piece of career advice ever, and that's to have a positive attitude. So much of being successful at work comes down to being likeable and friendly. And, of course, positive language is how you express that likeable, friendly, positive attitude! This is something they talk about a lot in the world of customer service, and the truth is that having a customer-service-esque attitude at work (no matter what you do or what industry you work in) will serve you well.

For example, say a leader in the company asks you to do something that's objectively not your job and that you don't even know how to do. Rude. Or maybe it's not rude, and she just doesn't know better and thinks this is what you do. You could say, 'That's not my job.' Sure, that might be technically true, but imagine that a few months later, that leader is hiring for an exciting role in her department. How will she remember you, or will she remember you at all?

I'm not saying that you have to say yes to all these types of requests. Boundaries are a good thing. But what if you used positive language and were helpful without doing the heavy lifting? For example, you could say, 'Oh, is that an invoice? I'd be happy to connect you with Sheri in accounting who handles that.' Boom. You were helpful and positive, and that leader is more likely to remember you, well... positively.

Here are a few more examples of how to use positive language:

'There's nothing I can do' becomes 'It's tough, but I'll work on finding a solution.'

'I don't know' becomes 'I'd be happy to look into that.'

REPLACE BACKWARD-FACING LANGUAGE WITH FORWARD-FACING LANGUAGE

Just like I encourage you to err on the positive, being proactive is also a surefire way to come off as more professional. You will sound more like a leader if you focus on the future instead of

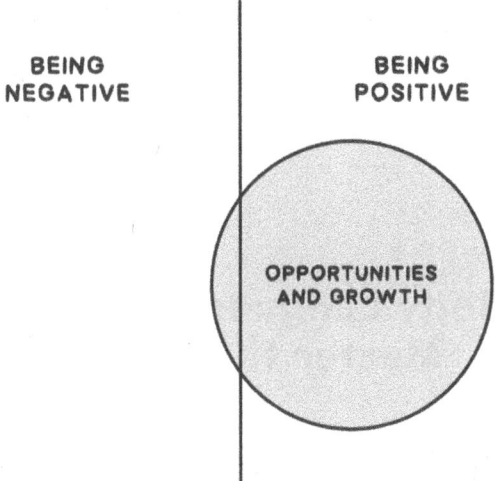

dwelling on the past. Try not to talk too much about what went wrong, and instead focus on what can be improved moving forward. Someone who thinks and talks this way is someone other people want to follow.

Once you start paying attention, you'll notice that the most charismatic leaders naturally tend to use forward-facing language. So why not be one of them? A simple reframing of your language to be proactive versus reactive puts you in the driver's seat and makes you sound like a true leader.

For example:

'Let's try this new method because things didn't work so well last time' becomes 'Let's try this new method to do things more effectively in the future.'

'Every time we work together, we get derailed by Carly and Martin fighting' becomes 'This time, we need to make sure everyone's voice is being heard.'

'For the past year, I've been totally overwhelmed by my workload, and I need more support' becomes 'Looking forward, I am going to need more support to help with my workload.'

Body Language: How to Master the Basics

Finally, we come to body language, an often overlooked but incredibly important ingredient in the recipe for professional communication.

In the 1960s, Albert Mehrabian was one of the first psychologists to study how much body language impacts our ability to communicate. He found that communication is made up of about 55 per cent nonverbal communication, 38 per cent vocal communication (meaning voice and tone), and only 7 per cent actual words alone.[1] While his research was merely the tip of the iceberg and these specific percentages have been disputed, the thesis rings true: Body language is way more important than most folks realize.

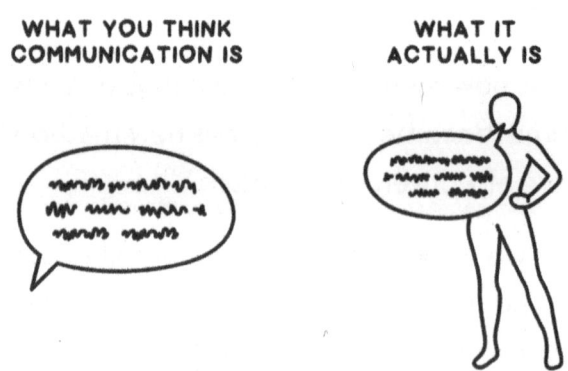

While I can and will tell you the best words to say in any situation, they are going to absolutely backfire if you don't use the right body language. Here are some foundational tips for basic body language that will help you ooze confidence and professionalism.

MAKE EYE CONTACT - BUT NOT TOO MUCH

Eye contact communicates a ton about what you're thinking and feeling and whether or not you're even paying attention to the other person. But it's important to strike the right balance. When you avoid eye contact, it may seem like you're distracted, disinterested or rude. On the other hand, staring intently into a colleague's eyes might lead them to report you to HR.

Eye contact has actually been studied extensively, and researchers have found that it's ideal to maintain eye contact for 50 per cent of the time while speaking and 70 per cent of the time while listening. Each time, maintain eye contact for about four to five seconds, then look off to the side, and then make eye contact again.[2] Make sure to use this as a general guide, though, rather than getting in your head and counting to four every time you make eye contact!

If this doesn't come naturally to you, you're not alone. Many of my friends who are neurodiverse struggle with eye contact. If this is you and you are scared you might come off as disinterested, feel free to politely disclose the reason for your limited eye contact: 'Hi, before we get started, I wanted to let you know sometimes it's hard for me to make eye contact. I don't want you to think I'm disinterested or distracted. I am very excited to be here today!'

One of my favourite tips for eye contact is to pretend the person you're talking to is a celebrity you're excited to meet – not a celebrity who's so famous that you'd be scared, but maybe someone you'd feel really comfortable with and look up to. If you feel this excitement in your body, you will naturally have better eye contact with the other person.

USE OPEN GESTURES

People love seeing your hands. They love seeing you gesture. They love seeing you illustrate what you're talking about. Vanessa Van Edwards is a body language expert, and in her book *Captivate* she writes about how gestures that align with verbal content can improve listener comprehension and retention. For instance, numerical gestures (e.g., showing three fingers when mentioning 'three points') reinforce spoken information – people love it.

Bottom line: You want to avoid keeping your hands hidden and keep them visible. If you're sitting at a table, always have your hands above the table, or people might subconsciously be distracted. You also want to avoid negative gestures like finger-pointing or quick, aggressive movements.

SMILE MORE

At the risk of sounding like a creepy dude on the street telling you that you'd look prettier if you smiled more . . . you should probably smile more. But not because you'd be prettier! It's a basic fact that humans are drawn to people who smile. This is also an important way for you to communicate your helpful and positive attitude.

Plus, smiling is contagious! The more you smile, the more the people around you will smile, and the better everyone will feel! As Maya Angelou said, 'People will forget what you said, people will forget what you did, but people will never forget how you made them feel.' Smile around them, and people will remember you fondly.

STAND UP STRAIGHT

Yes, your mother was right. Good posture is an important way to communicate your confidence. So stop slouching and straighten up that back! Right now, do it with me. Pull your shoulders up to your ears, back and down. Pretend there is a string tied from the top of your head to the ceiling. Engage your core (hello, Pilates friends!), relax your jaw, and lead with your sternum. This signals openness. And don't be afraid to take up space! Curling into yourself and literally making yourself small signals a lack of power, status and confidence, while opening up your stature is a classic power move. Good posture doesn't just make you look better – it is scientifically proven to make you feel better too.

BE A MIRROR

Humans naturally mimic the body language of the people they are speaking to. In fact, we have 'mirror neurons' in our brains that control this process. Evolutionarily speaking, this is a way of signalling to others that we are a member of the tribe, so they shouldn't, you know, kill us. In the workplace, mirroring accomplishes basically the same thing. When we mirror someone, they subconsciously assume that we have a lot in common. This makes them like us more because we're naturally drawn to those who are similar to us.

Thanks to those mirror neurons, many of us naturally copy each other's body language. If you start paying attention, you might notice yourself and others doing it. But if you don't already do this naturally, start to take note of how the people you're talking to are sitting or standing, and try positioning yourself similarly. The trick here is to do it subtly – not to overtly mimic them like an annoying little sister.

For example, if the person you're talking to leans back in their seat, wait a few moments and then lean back a tiny bit too. If they cross their legs, think about crossing yours. It should not be noticeable to the other person, but their subconscious mind will pick up on the mirror effect and assume good things about you.

You can also try verbal mirroring, which is a technique that involves repeating back the other person's phrases. This is actually a lot like active listening, and it has a similar effect. For example, if your colleague says, 'Our boss can be such a jerk sometimes,' you could just say, 'I know, right?' But if you say, 'I know, right? He *can* be such a jerk sometimes,' the mirroring effect will help build your connection.

This is one of those secret tricks that charismatic, powerful communicators use, and now that you know about it, you're going to see it everywhere. For example, if I'm talking to a charismatic person and I say, 'Sometimes I just feel like we're going one step forward and two steps back,' and they say, 'One step forward and two steps back – I understand completely,' it makes me feel good about myself! Like what I said was so great, they had to repeat it! This is a small trick you can use to make people fall in love with talking to you.

GREAT JOB! You now have a solid foundation of the right mindset and verbal and body language basics to supercharge your communication. Before we move on, take a moment to go back through and practise some of the tips with friends, but remember: Don't pick your nice friend, pick your honest friend!

Next up, we're going to talk about the secret language of written communication and reveal how successful people email differently from the rest of us.

CHAPTER 3

The Art of Written Communication

> If it is possible to cut a word out, always cut it out.
> —GEORGE ORWELL

Let's be honest, a huge percentage of your workplace communications won't be spoken in person, on the phone, or even over Zoom – it will be written. This aspect of the secret language of work is always changing. Just a few years ago, most written workplace communication took place over email, and most of the time it was pretty formal in tone. Now, many workplaces are embracing messaging services like Slack, Teams, Google Chat, or even text, and the tone of these messages is generally much more casual. However, not all workplaces are created equal, and culture around written communication at work can vary widely based on your industry and geography.

I always say that there are only two skills you truly need to master in order to be successful in any industry: writing and selling (both of which sit on the shoulders of the foundational skill of communication). We'll talk about selling when we discuss networking, interviews and negotiation in the next few chapters, but for now, we're going to focus on writing. If you can develop strong writing skills, you will inevitably rise up in the world.

Making mistakes in your written communication is a surefire way to look like a naive rookie. But most folks learn about things like email etiquette through embarrassing trial and error because there's no official training on written communication in the workplace. (Hello again, hidden curriculum.) Don't be the person who replies all to a company-wide email or sends long-winded, typo-ridden updates to clients. Upgrading your written communication game is the easiest way to elevate your status at work, increase your productivity, decrease miscommunication and get everyone to love you.

Which Format Should I Use?

Especially when you start a new job, it can be hard to know whether to hit someone up at work over Slack, text or email, because different workplaces and teams have their own cultures and preferences. As a freelancer, I've had to adapt to many different written communication styles based on the company I'm working for. Some were very buttoned up over email and some texted casually.

To communicate professionally, adaptation is key. Sorry, but you don't always get to do it your way. You may prefer to talk things through and avoid putting anything in writing altogether, but your company might use a specific software to track every detail of a project. Or you may prefer to communicate only via your work email, but your team constantly communicates on Slack. So when you're starting a job, pay attention to the forms of communication the people around you are using. If they are texting each other, don't write long-winded emails signed 'Most sincerely yours'. (Also don't write long-winded emails in general – more on that in a second.) If you're unsure, ask! When you're new to a job, there's no harm in simply asking how the team prefers to communicate.

As a general rule, written communication at work is for giving or asking for information. That's it. Don't try to brainstorm, engage in a debate or have a discussion in writing. One easy way to know which platform is best to communicate what you want to say is as simple as looking at the length of your message. A message that's one or two sentences can be a direct message (like Slack or Teams). A message that's two to ten sentences long should probably be an email. Anything longer than ten sentences should be a verbal conversation.

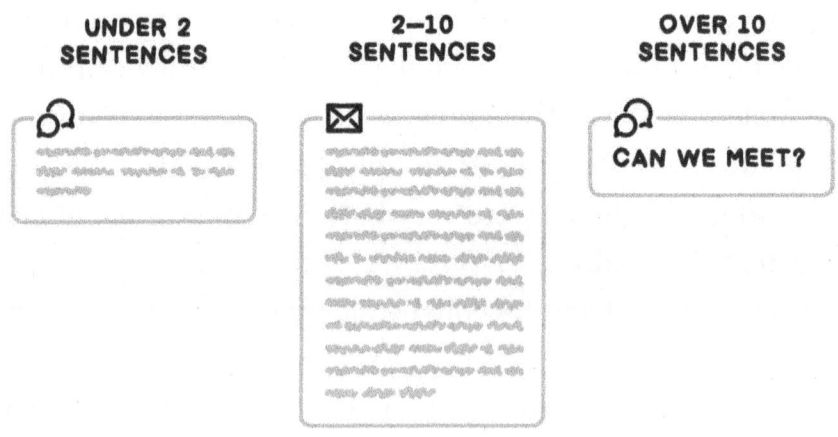

Also, pay attention to how long it is taking you to write a message. If you're spending more than five minutes crafting your message and/or you find yourself rewriting it a hundred times, pick up the phone and call instead. You can always follow up over email after the conversation if the topic is something you want to have in writing.

Five Steps to Writing Better Emails

Although email standards are always evolving, there are some tips for communicating over email at work that will never go out of style. Here are the five most important:

1. GET THE BASICS RIGHT

It may seem nitpicky, but it's worth taking the time to reread an email before sending it to make sure you got all the little things right. Did you spell the other person's name correctly? Is your grammar on point? (Pro tip: Download Grammarly for automatic grammar/spelling checks!) Did you reply all if you meant to, and did you definitely not reply all if you didn't mean to? If you're including a link, did you create a hyperlink instead of cutting and pasting a URL, which can look sloppy?

Writing thoughtful, well-written emails might feel time-consuming, but people appreciate it, and it adds up. And I know, I know – you might do all this work just for your fifty-five-year-old millionaire boss to respond, 'K. Sent from my iPhone.' But remember, they already put in the work. Do what you need to do and build up your status and reputation so that one day you'll be able to get away with writing 'K. Sent from my iPhone' too.

2. CREATE A PROFESSIONAL ADDRESS AND SIGNATURE

If you work at a corporation, 99 per cent of the time they will give you a professional company email account that you will use for all your work emails. However, you still need to have a personal email account that you can use when applying to jobs, emailing connections, following up, etc. You want to avoid having an unprofessional email address like virgokittylover420@yahoo.com or ilovemydog2020@hotmail.net. If your personal email address looks something like this, no judgement – we all had to make emails in middle school – but I suggest creating a new professional email address for yourself that you can use for anything work-related.

Likewise, make sure you have a simple, professional signature at the bottom of your email to bookend your messages. These are easy to set up in the settings section of your email provider. Avoid the 'Sent from my iPad' or having any graphic or quotes in your signature. (These are problematic for many reasons.)

That said, you can choose a sign-off that fits your personality. You don't have to end your emails with 'Yours sincerely' in order to be professional. 'Cheers', 'Best', 'Regards' and 'Warmly' are all fair game. Or you can mix it up and say 'Have a great Monday', or 'Have a great weekend', which can feel friendlier and more personal. However, maybe save 'XOXO' for emails to your mum and/or if you happen to be Gossip Girl. Hey, Upper East Siders!

3. CREATE CLEAR SUBJECT LINES

So much of good email communication comes down to being considerate of the person on the other end. We're all busy with overloaded inboxes, so make it easy for people to read, understand, and find your email among the chaos.

To start, make your subject line clear. For example, instead of 'Following up', try 'Following up | Invoice #2498'. Some companies label their emails with subjects like [Action Needed] or [Response Requested] so it's super clear what needs to be done. Eliminate guesswork! People tend to really appreciate this.

4. KEEP IT CONCISE

Everyone appreciates receiving well-edited emails that are easy to read and understand. In general, try cutting the length of your emails in half. Seriously. It's better to err on the side of being too concise than risk the recipient not reading your entire email because it's so long.

"UNDERSTOOD. THANKS."

"I DON'T HAVE TIME FOR THIS."

A great methodology for crafting concise emails is called BLUF. This is a communication hack that the military developed to literally save lives. It may not save your life, but it will prevent you from having to go back and forth with Karen from IT about thirty times to solve a simple server issue, and that's basically the same thing.

BLUF stands for 'Bottom Line Up Front'. It's very simple. You say the most important thing first and then add more context or caveats underneath. Most people do the opposite. They front-load with context and then get to the thesis, but this doesn't always make it clear to the reader what the takeaway or action items are. Here's an example:

Before BLUF:

Email – Hey Erin, how did the meeting go?

Email response – Well, at first we had some trouble logging in because Zoom was being finicky. And then one of their VPs joined. I think his name was Robert California? Then we did the presentation, but we didn't even end up showing them the 3rd option because they really liked the first two, and we're going to move forward with option 2. We are going to follow up. The meeting is next Wednesday at 10 a.m.

With BLUF:

Email – Hey Erin, how did the meeting go?

Email response – The meeting went really well. Here are three highlights:
1) Robert California, their VP of marketing joined.
2) We're moving forward with option #2.
3) We scheduled a follow-up for next Wednesday at 10 a.m.

Ah, doesn't that feel so much better? Efficiency, friends, we love to see it!

5. ESTABLISH YOUR TONE EARLY

Another important email tip is to establish your 'email voice' early on during your time with a company, and then make sure you stick with it. A lot of people start a job eager to please and write super-friendly, over-the-top emails with lots of exclamation points!!! This is understandable – we all want to make a good impression – but the problem here is that you are setting an expectation for your email tone. Then six months later when you fire off a quick email on your way to the airport with no exclamation points, people might read into the change of tone.

Keep your emails simple and straightforward from the beginning. It's okay to just write what you need to write. Here is an example of what *not* to do:

> Hi Kelly!!
>
> It's so nice to hear from you! Thanks for getting back to me so quickly! I'm sure you get requests like this all the time, so I'll keep this brief. Are you able to get on a call with Kevin tomorrow at 2pm? We just need to go over the timeline one more time, if you don't mind! Thanks again, Kelly!
>
> Best,
> Erin

Sure, that's one way you could send the email, but that takes a lot of calories to communicate something very simple. Instead, try something like this:

> Hi Kelly,
>
> Thanks for your quick response. Can Kevin get on a call tomorrow at 2pm to review the timeline?
>
> Erin

Short, polite and concise. People will not think you're mean if you set this standard first thing. But if you go from writing like the former to the latter overnight, people may raise eyebrows and question your mood. Who needs that?

The Email Scripts

Would I even be your favourite career advice friend if I didn't provide scripts for some common email topics, particularly around our favourite topic, job hunting? Let's get to it!

HOW TO WRITE A PREINTERVIEW EMAIL

If you're applying for a job you really want, I highly recommend emailing the interviewer before the interview. No, this is not annoying! It is actually really helpful. The person doing the interviewing is probably overwhelmed with candidates and can barely remember who is who. Reaching out beforehand to explain why you think you're a great fit for the role will help you stand out and also make the other person's job easier – win-win!

For example:

> Hi John,
>
> I'm Erin, and I'm really looking forward to my interview this Friday at noon for the role of Video Editor. Ahead of our conversation, I'd love to share three reasons I feel that I would be the perfect fit for this role:

1. I have a strong background (seven years of experience) in commercial video editing.
2. I am very collaborative, creatively curious and self-motivated.
3. I have additional skills in sound design, colour correction and audio editing.

I look forward to speaking with you on Friday!
Best,
Erin

HOW TO WRITE A FOLLOW-UP EMAIL

To answer your question, yes! You should absolutely, 100 per cent send a follow-up email after every single job interview you go on! It doesn't have to be complicated. Start by saying how great it was to meet the other person, and thank them for their time. Then reiterate your enthusiasm for the role and the fact that you believe you'd be a good fit. Finally, reference something you discussed during the interview and, if possible, attach some sort of relevant resource. This will help remind them of exactly who you are and add value.

For example:

Hi John,
It was great to meet you yesterday – thank you for taking the time. I really enjoyed hearing more about what CNBC is looking for in an Editor and am confident I'd be a

great fit for this role. After our conversation, I am even more excited at the opportunity to join the team and contribute my skills.

I know I briefly mentioned a Nike campaign I worked on, so I am attaching a link here for your convenience. It showcases my approach to sports editing, which I'm looking forward to diving into more in this role.

If you have any questions, please feel free to reach out anytime.

Best,

Erin

HOW TO WRITE A CHECK-IN EMAIL

When you haven't heard from a potential employer (or someone else you're waiting to hear from), you might start agonizing about when you should check in, if at all. You don't want to be annoying, and you might start telling yourself that it's pointless, because if they wanted to hire you, they probably would have reached out by now. But if done professionally, it's neither annoying nor pointless to check in. It's simply a chance to remind them of how great you are and hopefully get some information about the status of their search.

Start by saying that you're checking in to see if they have an update, and ask if there's anything else you can provide. Then reiterate why you'd be a great fit for the role and thank them for their time. And done – not annoying!

For example:

Hi Emily, it's Erin McGoff!

I interviewed for the Editor role on 3/5.

I'm checking to see if:

1. You have a status update on your hiring decision (or next steps).
2. There is any additional information I can provide to strengthen my application.

To reiterate, I believe I'd be a great fit for this role for these reasons:

1. I have seven years of professional commercial editing experience.
2. I am a culture fit – creatively curious, self-motivated, etc.
3. I have the additional skills you're seeking (sound editing in particular).

Thank you so much, Emily!
I look forward to hearing from you.
Best,
Erin

Pro tip? Say people's names! Especially over email, it's great to add a bit more humanity to our cyber communications. People love seeing their own name. Just make sure it's spelled correctly!

HOW TO RESPOND TO A REJECTION EMAIL

What? You don't respond to rejection emails? That's one of my favourite pastimes! Okay, but real talk: Learning how to professionally respond to rejection is part of the secret language of work. If you get a rejection, do not – I repeat, do not – leave their email unread. Also, do not give a snarky response like, 'k' or 'Whatever, didn't really want it anyway, so...' I know it's tempting. But resist!

You may be shocked to hear that responding to a rejection email can change the trajectory of your entire career. You never know when this person will be in a position to hire or help you again, and it's both professional and in your best interest to leave things on a positive note. Also, you'd be surprised by how often the person they hire doesn't work out and they have to revisit the candidate pool. Thank them, express your disappointment as well as your gratitude for being considered, and think about asking for feedback that you can use in the future.

For example:

Dear Katie,

Thank you for taking the time to let me know and for considering my application.

While I am very disappointed, I very much enjoyed getting to meet you and learn more about a career at HBO.

Would you be willing to provide feedback on what I could improve on? (Don't worry, it won't hurt my feelings. I welcome feedback!)

I hope our paths cross again soon, and I wish you all the best moving forward.

Best,

Erin

ALL RIGHT, now that we have the basics down, we are going to move on to the specific workplace scenarios and more detailed scripts to help you communicate your way to the career of your dreams.

CHAPTER 4

Network Without Cringing

Opportunities do not float like clouds in the sky. They are attached to people.

—RICH STROMBACK

In this chapter, we're going to talk all about networking. Wait, wait – don't put down the book, no! Stay with me here! Networking gets a bad rap, and I honestly feel bad for her. If you learn how to network correctly it will be neither painful nor awkward, neither uncomfortable nor cringe. I promise.

What holds so many people back from networking is fear – fear of being too forward, fear of feeling awkward, or fear of causing offence to others while embarrassing themselves. It feels safer to just stay home, keep our mouths shut, and let people come to us, right? Well, I have some bad news for you: That is a great recipe for a tremendously mediocre career. I can't stress this enough: If you want to have a successful career, land a job you love, make a lot of money and feel fulfilled, you need to learn the skill – nay, the art – of talking to other people. And that's really all that networking is.

Have you ever wondered how certain folks get amazing jobs?

You know, the ones with great work-life balance, cool coworkers, plenty of vacation, great pay and good benefits? It's networking. It's not just about what you know, it's about who you know. And it's not just about who you know, but who you know knows. And it's not just about who you know knows, but who you know knows knows you. I think we're on the same page.

This chapter isn't about standing around in a giant fluorescent conference room wearing a name tag while holding a Styrofoam cup of coffee and trying to balance a tiny plate of cheese cubes and crackers while you shake someone's hand. I mean, yes, that is one form of networking – and if you enjoy it, bless. But it's not the only way. I am about to introduce you to an entirely new brand of networking that might even be, dare I say, kind of fun? (And yes, even for my fellow introverts and small-talk haters, you're going to love this.)

The Hidden Job Market

Before we dive into networking, I need to introduce you to a little thing called the hidden job market, which consists of jobs that are secured through connections. Research shows that as many as 85 per cent of all jobs are filled through the hidden market.[3] If you feel like sometimes your job applications vanish into the void, that's because they probably do. And someone else with a connection got the role. Is it fair? No. But it's reality.

Companies prefer hiring someone with a personal referral over a stranger, because if you have a connection, you've already been vetted. It's like dating. Would you rather go out with a random dude bro you found online, or your friend's hot coworker who she swears is your dream man? Case closed. Besides, hiring is expensive and time-consuming. Companies much prefer promoting internally or hiring through word of mouth over launching full job searches.

Here's a real-life example: When I left my full-time job in 2022, the first thing the company asked me was 'Do you know anyone who could replace you?' Even if they had to post the job online for compliance, they'd be more likely to pick my referral over an unknown applicant. They'd rather hire another Erin, and they figured the best person to find one was ... Erin.

This happens everywhere every day. To put yourself in the running for the jobs in the hidden job market, people need to know you and be willing to speak your name in a room full of possibilities. And the best way to make this happen is to build

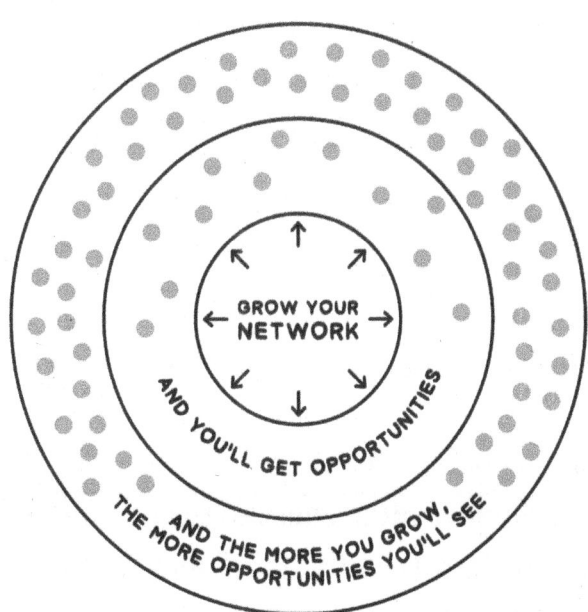

your network while being a likeable, capable professional whom others are proud to vouch for.

In this chapter, I'll break networking down into three categories: who (peer or reach networking), where (online or in-person), and how (in or out of context). We already know what (networking, duh), when (always), and why (to get in the cool kids' hidden job market club).

Who: Reach Versus Peer Networking

REACH NETWORKING

Reach networking is when you connect with someone who is 'above' you, meaning they are more experienced, older and/or more senior, like your boss, a mentor or a professor. A rookie mistake that many make when attempting reach networking is only reaching out (get it?) when they need something, like a job or advice. But networking isn't about taking; it's about connecting.

So, step one to reach networking is just to connect. Find someone you have some link to, even a small one – they work at your company, you see them at networking events, you follow their content. Don't ask for anything. Introduce yourself and perhaps offer a personalized compliment. That's it.

Yes, senior people are likely able to help you, but for that reason they're swamped with requests. I get countless messages asking for 'a quick call', and I ignore most of them. It sounds harsh, but when you receive dozens of messages every single week from strangers who just want things from you, you have to ignore them for the sake of your boundaries. But if someone reaches out with 'Hi Erin! I love your videos – here's an article you might like,' I notice.

This all goes back to a psychological theory known as the reciprocity principle, which Adam Grant, an organizational psychologist and Wharton School of Business professor, writes about in his book *Give and Take*. The reciprocity principle describes the human tendency to return a favour or kindness. But it isn't a hard-and-fast rule. Reciprocity isn't one to one, but rather an implied, well, give-and-take. Good title.

Be aware of this concept, but don't try to use it to manipulate. If someone gives with an agenda, we're less likely to want to return the favour than we are when someone is genuine and helps without expecting anything in return. If you plant enough seeds, a few flowers are bound to bloom.

As the relationship grows, continue to offer value. Send useful articles, share the other person's posts, buy and review their book, and/or congratulate them on accomplishments. These small actions help build the connection. Then when you eventually need something, the other party will be more inclined to help with small favours (ideally something that can be done in less than thirty seconds) because the relationship is genuine.

For example, when I was starting out in film, I admired a director named Anne and dreamt of her being my mentor. I didn't ask her for anything, but I supported her. I attended her premieres, wrote positive reviews, liked her posts, and congratulated her on her wins. Over time, she noticed. One day, when I faced a tough challenge directing a short film, I emailed her and asked for advice. She not only replied, but called me within minutes.

I never asked Anne to be my mentor, and don't you go asking people this either. Focus on building the relationship, and over time you'll naturally develop a mentor-mentee dynamic. And don't be afraid to aim high! Reach out to the CEO or the star in your field. High-level professionals appreciate boldness.

Wondering how to reach them? Social media (public accounts) or LinkedIn are fair game. To find their emails, tools like RocketReach or ContactOut work. But don't spam – use this info wisely and with respect. To start, you can try a simple LinkedIn message like this, and build from there:

> Hi Jeff!
>   My name is Erin McGoff, and I'm a video editor in NYC. I saw you speak on the panel at Sundance and loved your thoughts on the future of SVOD. Would love to connect.
>   Erin

PEER NETWORKING

Peer networking is connecting with someone who's on the same level as you. Maybe you're around the same age, in similar roles, with similar ambitions. These are people in the same boat as you, and you are equally positioned to help each other.

Many people overlook the importance of peer networking, but it's invaluable. Think of your reach contacts as the army generals and your peer contacts as your comrades. The generals will pop in every now and then, but your fellow soldiers are the ones who are in the trenches with you day in and day out. They get it and can share tips, ideas and opportunities.

Plus, peers won't stay peers forever. Today's intern could be tomorrow's VP. This is one reason you should never burn bridges. The world is much smaller than you think it is. Your peers are also connected to people you aren't – yet. Expanding your peer network multiplies your overall reach.

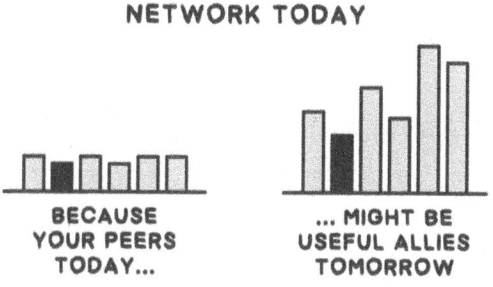

Where: Online Versus In-Person Networking

ONLINE NETWORKING

Introverts, I have some good news: We are living in the best time in human history for you when it comes to work in general and networking in particular. The internet has made it so that you can sit on your couch in your pyjamas with messy hair and your laptop open and network without having to talk to a single person. Heaven! This also makes networking a lot easier if you live in a remote area without a lot of opportunities to network in person.

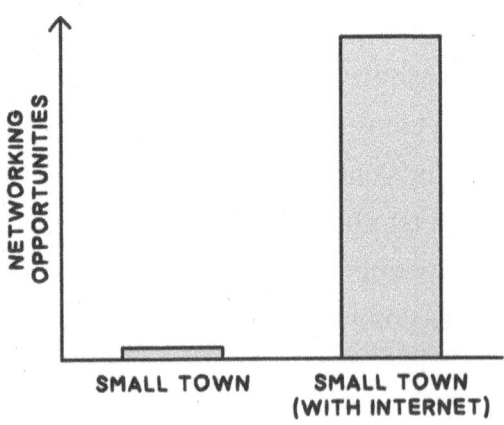

As you likely know, online networking is all about connecting to people over email, social media and LinkedIn. If you're not already on LinkedIn, make yourself a profile right now. While LinkedIn is more useful for some industries than others, in general it's an incredibly powerful networking tool for everyone. LinkedIn doesn't have to be intimidating. Simply set up your profile, upload a photo, write your tagline, fill out some work experience and you're good to go. Seriously, I'll wait. Once you're ready, there are two kinds of online networking: warm outreach and cold outreach.

Warm Outreach

This is when you reach out to someone online that you have some type of existing connection with. Maybe you have a mutual friend or worked for the same company or went to the same college or university. Basically, you have something in common, and you want to leverage that commonality to connect with this person.

Having something in common with a potential connection

multiplies your chances of successfully forming that relationship by a factor of a lot. Again, it goes back to ancient times. If someone walked into your village and said, 'Hi, I'm Fred,' you'd be like, 'Wait, who are you?' But if someone walked into your village and said, 'Hi, I'm Fred, I'm friends with Barney,' you might be like, 'Oh, I love Barney! Welcome in, want some stew?'

So if there's someone you'd like to network with, first do a little snooping to figure out if you can turn it into a warm connection. This is one reason LinkedIn is so handy. Say you heard someone in your industry being interviewed on a podcast and you want to connect. You hop onto LinkedIn and scour their profile to see if you have something in common. Lo and behold, you have a mutual connection. Then you can email the following:

Dear Michael,
   It appears we both know Dwight Schrute! He was my boss when I worked at Schrute Farms. How do you two know each other? I wanted to reach out because I heard you on the *Scranton Times* podcast, and I loved what you had to say about the future of the paper industry. I'm looking forward to staying connected.
   Best,
   Erin

Michael is going to be so much more likely to respond to your email because of your mutual connection via Dwight. And now Michael is part of your network. Nice!

Because people are more responsive to warm outreach, it's a good idea to try to increase your number of warm connections. One way to do this is by joining an affiliate group. For example, when I was in college I joined the sorority Chi Omega. I know, I know, did you peg me to be a sorority girl?

I never expected to be the kind of person who joined a sorority. (No offence to sororities, but I had little exposure to what they were outside of Delta Nu in *Legally Blonde*.) But when I met this group of women during my first semester at American University I said, 'Sign me up!' Now, whenever I apply for a job, I search LinkedIn to see if there are any Chi Os at that company. Even if I don't know them personally, our mutual affiliation gives me a great excuse to spark a conversation with them.

For example:

Hi Alex!

My name is Erin McGoff. I was a Chi Omega (Eta Lambda chapter) at American University. I'm reaching out because I see you work at HBO, and I'm considering applying for the Video Editor position there. Do you enjoy working at HBO? Would you recommend it as a good place to work? Thank you!

Erin

Even though Alex and I do not know each other and have no mutual friends, we now have an established connection through our shared experience of being part of the same organization. You probably already belong to groups you can leverage. This doesn't have to be Greek life! They tend to be based on shared values or interests. For example, your religious affiliation, alma mater, running club, volunteer organization, internship, country of origin, neighbourhood, cause you support, etc. all count as affiliate groups.

Besides affiliate groups, there are plenty of ways to warm up your connections. For example, someone recently reached out to me on my public Instagram account about how she thought my rescue dog, Olive, was so cute and kind of looked like her rescue, Minnow. She attached an adorable photo. How could I resist that? She established a connection through our mutual passion for rescue dogs. All she had to do was look at my social media and find my soft spot.

Find something the person you're trying to connect with is genuinely passionate about and start the conversation there. Pro tip? If someone has a pet or kids, that's almost a guaranteed way in. Tell them that their kids and/or pets are adorable, and you're off to a great start. But tread lightly with the kid thing. Don't come off creepy or disingenuous, please.

Cold Outreach

Cold outreach, on the other hand, is when you've got nothing to go on. You're sending a random person a random message. You've sleuthed and come up dry – no mutual connections, companies, education, interests, nada. It's like you're from two different planets.

It can feel scary to make the first move with a complete stranger, but remember, this is what networking is all about! Plus, there is literally no risk here. If you cold email someone, the worst-case scenario is that they don't ever respond. Not the end of the world. I mean, I guess they could respond, 'Why are you such a weirdo reaching out to someone you don't know? Never contact me again. #Blocked.' But that's unlikely.

That said, you're probably going to have to work a little bit harder to stand out and get a response from a cold outreach, especially if the other person is a reach connection. Likely, the person you're reaching out to is busy and isn't going to respond to every 'Hey, I'd love to connect' email he or she receives. There are a few ground rules that are important to follow here:

First, keep your message short. So short! No more than five sentences, max. Second, rely on good old-fashioned flattery, and be specific (and genuine!). For example, if I were to message a filmmaker, I would mention that I saw their most recent film and really liked how they did this one specific thing. This makes it feel more personal and lets the other person know that you're not just cutting and pasting the same message to a million different people. (Also, don't do that.)

I can vouch for this from the other side of the table too. When someone messages me saying they really like how I do a certain thing in my videos, it shows me that this person actually engages with and cares about my content. They took time to reach out to me, so I am more likely to take time responding to them. (Hello, reciprocity principle, we meet again!)

Finally, as I mentioned earlier, find a way to add value. For example, one of my followers recently emailed me to pitch herself as my virtual assistant. In her email, she said that she had already gone through my entire website, and she included a list of typos she'd found. I wasn't offended – I was impressed! That took time and truly added value. Sadly, I wasn't looking for a virtual assistant at the time, but if I was, she would have been at the top of my list. And if I ever am in the future, I know exactly who to contact.

Your first point of contact should look something like this:

Subject: Hi [their name], I'm [your name]
Hello! My name is [your name] and I'm a [profession] in [location]. I'm reaching out to [give them a sincere compliment and/or provide value to them]. I'd love to connect with you here. I hope to cross paths sometime in the future. Have a great [day of the week/weekend/week]!
[Your name]

Then, if they reply with 'Thank you', or 'Good to get connected', then great! Don't expect them to reply offering to grant you three wishes. If they heart your message, that's also a win. Later on, you can follow up with a more specific ask.

For example, if you are looking for a job, and they are a hiring manager, try something like:

Hi [their name],
You're welcome! It's great to get connected. How are things going at HBO? I'm exploring the idea of pursuing a career there as an Editor. If you're hiring anytime in the future, I'd love to be considered. I'm happy to send over my résumé and portfolio if it's helpful.
Thank you! Erin

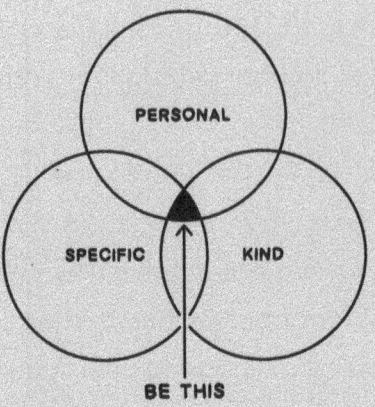

ONLINE NETWORKING WITH RECRUITERS AND HIRING MANAGERS

Let's get something straight: If someone is a recruiter or a hiring manager, it's literally their job to find quality people to fill open positions. A professional, successful recruiter will never be annoyed to be contacted by a potential candidate. It makes their job easier when you come to them.

So the rules of engagement when networking with these folks are a little bit different. In this case, the simple act of reaching out to them is providing value. If they're looking for a video editor and you reach out saying you're a video editor, you've saved them the time it would have taken to do research looking for a video editor. That's value added.

For this reason, most recruiters and hiring managers appreciate receiving cold emails when they're relevant and appropriate. Even if you're not the right fit for a position that's open right now, it's great for them to have your name on file so they can circle back to you when there's another opening. (Check out that jargon, y'all.) Plus, any good professional recruiter will appreciate you for taking the initiative.

However, when most people network with recruiters and hiring managers, they make the mistake of coming in way too hot. They say something like 'Hi, can you please look at my résumé? I saw there was an open role and wanna apply – Carrie.' That's like going on a first date and saying, 'So when would you like to get married?' Don't be so thirsty. You're not desperate – you're in demand! Reel it back a bit and try this instead:

'Hi, I'm Carrie, a San Francisco–based graphic designer with seven years of experience. I just applied for the graphic designer position at BuzzFeed, and I wanted to put a face to an application. Thank you so much for your consideration, and I look forward to hearing from you.'

That's it. You made your connection, and you showed that you're professional, personable and proactive. It's just a little cherry on top of your application, which can really help you stand out.

It's also a good idea to network with recruiters and hiring managers even when they don't have an open position available – or when you're not sure if they do – and say that you're interested in learning about pursuing a career at the company. Then you'll be top of mind when a position becomes available. Start by making a list of ten to twenty companies that you might want to work at, regardless of whether or not they have any job listings at the moment. (Remember that hidden job market!) Then message recruiters at the companies saying:

'Hi, my name is Carrie. I'm a San Francisco–based graphic designer with seven years of experience. I'm a big fan of your company and the work that you're doing. I'm happy to be connected.'

This is a great cold email because you're not directly asking for anything. You're just expressing your interest and kicking off a relationship with the company. Now they know you exist, and you're one step closer to having a powerful network.

IN-PERSON NETWORKING

As wonderful as online networking is, in-person networking is where the magic really happens. Just like with dating, where there is only so far swiping right and left can take you. There is just no replacement for meeting someone in real life and looking them in the eye while you interact.

If your palms are getting a little sweaty just thinking about pulling this off, don't worry!

I personally self-identify as a curious introvert who loathes small talk and conversation starters like 'So, what do you do for work?' The following are techniques I've personally used to navigate in-person networking with ease, mastery and, most important, success.

Before you head out to that next networking event, it's important to have your 'elevator pitch' ready. An elevator pitch is basically a little spiel you have prepared to tell people who you are and what you're all about. It's like your dating profile for the working world. It doesn't have to be complicated or long. In fact, it should be super short and sweet. Your elevator pitch should be just a couple of sentences that help people immediately understand your goals and how they might be able to help you reach them. Or as I like to say, speaking what you want into existence.

Imagine someone going to a networking event and meeting someone who says, 'Hi, I'm Lacy, and I'm a fourth-grade teacher.' Okay . . . that's cool! But it doesn't give you much information besides what Lacy currently does for work. Maybe if you ended up having a lengthy conversation with Lacy, you would eventually figure out a way to connect with her and help her. But that might never happen, and her intro doesn't give us much to work with.

Of course, this means you have to know what your goals are to begin with so you can communicate them clearly to others. Once you do, don't be afraid to say them out loud and be specific. Speak it into existence, people! Give the person you're talking to something to work with.

My formula for an elevator pitch is past + present + future:

- Where did you come from?
- What are you currently doing?
- And where do you want to go?

For example, imagine that Lacy says, 'Hi, I'm Lacy. I'm a fourth-grade teacher in the Dallas area. I'm currently enrolled in a master's program in educational leadership, and my goal is to become an elementary school principal within the next five years.' Okay, Lacy, pop off! Now we're getting somewhere.

Talking about your goals and where you see yourself going makes it clear how others can help you. It also helps you come across as a moving train – someone with momentum. You're moving forward with or without this person, and they're more than welcome to come along for the ride.

People naturally have an aversion to 'parked trains', or those who don't seem to know where they're going. People don't like to hear, 'I don't know what I'm doing with my life.' To be frank, it's boring to talk to someone who is confused and unmotivated. Pick a goal to focus on. You don't have to be glued to your destination or attached to a certain outcome. But you should be committed to the journey. Confidently stating your goals makes you seem competent and likeable. So do that.

Now that you've got your elevator pitch down, let's talk about the two ways you can network in person, which are in and out of context.

HOW TO GET BETTER AT SMALL TALK

Let's have a small talk about small talk. Oh, you don't like small talk? You think small talk is silly, boring and exhausting? Well, buckle up, buster, because I'm generally a pretty happy-go-lucky girl, but I'm about to hit you with some tough love.

Get over it. You don't hate small talk. You're just not good at small talk, and you don't understand the dire importance of mastering this social skill. Research shows that regularly making small talk actually makes you happier and that strategically engaging in small talk endears you to others.[4]

If you're reading this thinking, 'Well actually, Erin, I quite enjoy small talk, and I think I am pretty good at it,' I apologize for the aforementioned tough love. You are an anomaly and can probably skip this part.

For the rest of us, you should know that small talk is a skill that is part of the hidden curriculum and a big part of the secret language of work. So it's okay if you don't currently possess this skill. Plus, humans have become less social and more isolated, and many of us don't really know how to speak to one another anymore IRL without a keyboard barrier.

To improve your small talk, think of it as playing hacky sack. You know, that game they always show twentysomethings playing on the lawn of their liberal arts college in movies, but for some reason we never see outside that context. You want to kick the hacky sack a few times yourself and then bounce it back to the other person. Then let them kick it a few times before kicking it back to you. It's a give-and-take. You want to receive, expand and then throw it back.

For example:

Coworker: Good morning.

You: Good morning! [You receive.] How was your weekend? [You throw back.]

Coworker: It was good, how was yours?

You: It was good, thanks. [You receive.] My sister was in town, so I got to show her around my neighbourhood. [You expand.] What about you? Did you get to do anything fun? [You throw it back.]

Coworker: Oh, not really. I mean, I mulched my backyard, which I guess is kind of fun.

You: Oh, that's so cool that you have a backyard. [You receive.] I'm still in an apartment. But I hope to have a backyard for my dog someday. [You expand and gently throw back.] (Note: You don't always have to drill with questions. A simple pause to let the other person respond makes the conversation less exhausting for you.)

Coworker: Oh, what kind of dog do you have?

You: She's a rescue. Her name is Olive. Here's a picture. Do you have a dog? [You throw back.]

Coworker: Yeah, we have a goldendoodle named Waffles.

You: Oh, so cute, they both have food names! Well, I gotta run, but I'll see you at the quarterly.

Don't be afraid to end the conversation after two or three minutes. It is small talk, after all! Use a polite reason to excuse yourself. Here are some ideas:

- 'Well, I'd better get back to work. I'll see you at the all hands later?'

- 'I'm gonna go grab a coffee, but it was great talking to you.'

- 'I'm gonna let you get on with your day, but it was great catching up.'

See how easy that was? That last one is my favourite. If you're in a conversation where someone is going on way too long, just hit them with, 'Well, I'll let you go,' or 'I'll let you get on with your day, but it was great to catch up!' and exit.

To practise your small talk, go ride in some elevators. Compliment someone on their jacket, and ask them where they got it. Practise maintaining a conversation for thirty to sixty seconds and embracing silence. Smile! Then as the elevator doors ding and

> they prepare to get off, confidently say, 'Have a good one!' Once you've established this skill and strengthened this muscle, you'll see how much brighter a little small talk can make your day.

How: In-Context Networking

Let's go back to that big conference room with the cheese cubes just for a second. I promise we don't have to stay long! This type of environment is a classic example of what I call in-context networking: Professionals gather in a physical space for a conference, meetup or convention with the specific goal of meeting people in their industry or occupation.

These are great places to connect with people because everyone is there with the same intention. They're open to connecting with you because they're there specifically to connect. It's kind of like speed dating in a professional context. It can be very efficient! However, it can also be very scary, especially if you're just starting out.

The big question is, how can you strike up a conversation with someone at an in-context networking event without dying inside? This can feel so awkward. You know you're both there to network, but . . . how? How do you not just walk up to someone and word vomit, 'Hi, my name is project manager I am an

Erin, how do you do'? Fear not – I'm going to teach you my four top tips right now:

1. GET ON THE SAME PAGE

Have you ever started a conversation with someone and suddenly forgotten all the words in the English language? Remember: Small talk is a learned skill! It's okay if you don't know what to say next and, in fact, I made up a little acronym to help you keep the conversation flowing when your mind goes blank.

Just remember PAGE. It stands for 'Place, Activity, Goals, Exit'. This can help you maximize the conversation in a natural way, and one that will impress your conversation partner. For example, if you see someone standing alone by the coffee machine, walk up to them and confidently introduce yourself: 'Hi, I'm Tim, what's your name?' After you exchange names and maybe a little background information about where you work, try using PAGE:

Place: Have you ever been to Vegas before?
Activity: Did you see the keynote this morning?
Goals: Do you have any goals for the week, or are you just here to have fun?
Exit: Well, I have to go meet up with my coworker, but it was so nice to meet you!

Don't just bust out all these questions at once. Use them as needed to keep the conversation going. Of course, if the conversation starts to go naturally, you can let go of this script and just let it flow. But it can definitely come in handy if you're struggling to make conversation or just need an opener!

2. BE A MIRROR

Earlier, I mentioned the fact that if your body language and speech are similar to those of the person you're talking to, they will subconsciously like you more. When networking, try to match their energy too. For example, if the person you're talking to is analytical and low energy, don't come into the conversation as the most overcaffeinated and bubbly version of yourself. Instead, you want to tap into your analytical, chill side.

I know this may sound psychopathic, and honestly, it is, lol. Psychopaths are typically super charismatic! They know that mirroring supercharges their likeability and helps them literally get away with murder. So, you know, use these techniques to make new industry contacts, and not to kill innocent people.

3. BE INTERESTED AND BE INTERESTING

David Ogilvy, the original Mad Man who founded one of the most successful advertising agencies in the world, had a mantra: 'If you want to be interesting, be interested.'

Want to be liked? Ask people about themselves. People love to talk about themselves. I have entire conversations with people and walk away knowing nearly everything about them and them knowing nearly nothing about me, and they're probably thinking, 'I sure do like that Erin girl!'

The best way to chat people up at networking events is to ask thoughtful questions. Be genuinely curious, and remember that you can learn something from anyone. Try to listen more than you speak. Ask a question, and then share a little about yourself after they respond. Remember the hacky sack, and find a balance so that you both walk away feeling like you learned something about the other person and were also heard.

In addition to being interested, you also need to be interesting. There is nothing more boring than talking to someone who doesn't contribute to the conversation. I want to hear your hot takes, unpopular opinions, likes and dislikes. Have strong opinions, loosely held. Have hobbies, a favourite TV show you're bingeing, a trip coming up that you need advice on, and so on!

People like those who are decisive, opinionated and invested in a conversation. Simply knowing what you like or don't like (and why you like it or don't like it) will make you more interesting and give you an easy way to talk about yourself without bragging or seeming forced. Plus, when you know who you are and what you're into, you feel more confident.

For example, I love asking people, 'Do you have a current obsession?' Or, 'Are you watching any good shows? I need a recommendation for this weekend!' Having answers to questions like this ready to go will make you a more interesting and memorable person to network with. Feel free to say something unique! 'Honestly, I know it's not work related, but I've been rereading the Harry Potter series and that's my current obsession! Rereading your favourite childhood books as an adult is so fun.'

You can also make yourself interesting by wearing something that people can comment on – like a unique accessory or item of clothing. These are called conversation pieces for a reason.

They give people an excuse to strike up a conversation. Bonus points if this piece is something you got on a cool trip or there's a funny story attached to it that you can share.

4. FOLLOW UP

I always say, a networking bid doesn't truly count until you follow up. As with everything, solidify it in writing! When you get home from the event, look up everyone you met on LinkedIn and add them as a connection. But don't stop there. Send them a quick message to confirm the connection. If possible, reference something that you discussed to remind them who you are. Keep it short and sweet.

For example:

Dear Shannon,

It was so nice to meet you at the Tribeca Film Festival. I really enjoyed our conversation and will never forget your story about ice fishing in Vermont! I hope our paths cross again soon.

Best,
Erin

How: Out-of-Context Networking

Have you ever randomly made a work contact at a friend's birthday party, on an airplane, at the dog park, or anywhere else outside a professional workspace or networking event? If so, then you've engaged in what I call out-of-context networking. If in-context networking is like speed dating, out-of-context networking is like randomly meeting someone at a bar – organic, authentic, and easy!

Most folks focus on in-context networking, which is absolutely worthwhile. But in my opinion, the real juicy connections are made out of context. Why, you ask? When people aren't in their official professional environments, they let their guard down. This makes them more receptive and open to connecting with you.

For example, let's say David has a small start-up selling accounting software. He emails a senior vice president of a company he wants to pitch:

Dear Stacy,
My name is David, and I'm the founder of a new company called Account.io, supplying streamlined accounting software that is specifically designed for wholesale corporations at a fraction of the cost. Can I send you more information?
Thank you,
David

Stacy sees the email come into her inbox, opens it and clicks delete. It's a great cold email, but she's busy! She gets tons of pitches every single week, and David's email gets dumped into her trash with the rest of them.

However, let's say David goes with his girlfriend to her cousin's wedding. During cocktail hour, his girlfriend's parents casually introduce him to their lifelong friend Stacy.

Stacy takes a sip of her cocktail and shakes David's hand. 'It's nice to meet you, David! And what do you do for work?'

Pause, did she just ask how David makes money right out of the gate? Of course, she did! Stacy is speaking the secret language of work and treats everything as a networking opportunity. Sure, David could humble mumble, 'Oh, I just do accounting stuff, super boring,' because he doesn't want to risk sounding braggy. Or David could remember what I taught him: that the secret language is all about confidently and graciously sharing what you're working on. This is how successful people operate – they resist the urge to make themselves small.

'Oh, I actually am the founder of a start-up, Accounting.io, which streamlines accounting software, specifically designed for wholesale corporations,' David says. He's half expecting Stacy to say, 'Oh. Sounds boring. I'm going to try some of the shrimp cocktail, bye!'

Instead, she raises her eyebrows and says, 'Oh, wow! I actually run the East Coast division of Wholesale, Inc.' Bingo.

'What a coincidence,' David replies, trying to temper his enthusiasm. I mean, he came to this wedding as a random plus one; what are the chances he runs into an ideal client who could make or break his young start-up? 'I know we're here to have fun, but I'd love to stay connected with you,' David says, remembering to keep things light and save a hard ask or pitch for later.

'Sure, that'd be great. Here's my email address,' Stacy says and shares her contact information. She looks at David's girlfriend and her parents and says, 'See you on the dance floor,' and walks away.

The only difference in these two scenarios is the context in which David and Stacy meet. Instead of being in her office wearing a stuffy suit and stressed about supply-chain delays, Stacy is at a wedding wearing sandals and drinking a Tanqueray and tonic. And David isn't just a random MBA in her inbox. He's a friendly, nice-seeming, real-life guy who's dating her lifelong friends' sweet daughter – he's been vetted!

Stacy is now a solid contact. And even if David and Stacy don't end up working together, Stacy is likely to tell her tennis partner and PTA friend about David's company, and his web will continue to grow.

While Stacy is a reach contact for David, out-of-context networking also works with peers. For peer out-of-context networking, it really comes down to being friendly to the people you meet. Chat up your neighbours while checking your mailbox or while in your apartment building's laundry room. Engage in conversation with your fellow dog owners at the local dog park. After covering pleasantries, try asking them, 'So, what do you do for work?' Don't forget to have your elevator pitch ready to go. Tell people who you are and where your train is headed.

To seek out opportunities for out-of-context reach networking, you may have to get a little creative. Put yourself where powerful people hang out. This can be driving for Uber or Lyft in the financial district of New York City, picking up a golf caddy gig at the country club on the posh side of town, bartending at an upscale restaurant geared for postwork happy hours, or dog sitting or babysitting in an upper-class neighbourhood. Lovingly caring for a Fancy Company's Vice President of Everything's precious goldendoodle can get your foot in a very hard-to-open door.

NOW THAT YOU are a master networker, opportunities to interview for exciting roles are bound to start coming your way! Hello, hidden job market. So, next up we're going to tackle all things job interview so you can walk into these rooms with confidence, professionalism and poise.

CHAPTER 5

The Hidden Etiquette of Interviews

It's not about having the right opportunities. It's about handling the opportunities right.

—MARK CUBAN

Throughout your career, one of the most common and stressful scenarios you'll find yourself in is (dun, dun, dun) a job interview. 'Hello, we'd like to bring you in for an interview...' Just that sentence alone has my palms sweating and my heart fluttering.

Interviews are weird. They are thirty minutes to an hour of you sitting in a room and trying not to appear nervous while getting judged on every word you say (or don't say) and every movement you make (or don't make) – all to determine whether or not you will be picked for a job that pays for your survival. Plus, you can be the perfect fit for the role and still bomb the interview simply due to your anxiety about bombing the interview. The irony!

The truth is that being fluent in the secret language of work is never more important than it is in a job interview, and this chapter has got you covered. We'll start with some tips on how to combat anxiety and go from an anxious, nauseous, panicky candidate to a calm, relaxed, confident and self-assured professional. Then we'll tackle scripts for how to answer any type of question they might throw at you like a pro.

Battling Preinterview Anxiety

Picture this: You walk into a conference room with a few windows, fluorescent lighting and a long glass table. At the end of the table sit two hiring managers with suits on and laptops in front of them. 'Hi, you must be...' They reach out to shake your hand, and you freeze, thinking, *I must be... who? Who is me? What is name? I need to call my mum.* The panic sets in. *I shouldn't be here. I'm just wasting their time. They're going to hate me.* Your face gets hot and your hands clam up.

This used to be me. I haven't always been the articulate and confident professional you see today (flips hair, sips coffee). I know what it feels like to think, *Oh no, can they see that my face is getting super red? They totally can! Oh no, now my voice is shaking. It's getting worse – ah!*

Over the years, I interviewed more and more, and the nerves dulled and dulled. That's because interviewing is a skill, and the more you do it, the easier it gets. Not only will you get used to the interview setting and process with increased exposure, but as your career progresses, you will also feel more and more confident. You will have more stories to tell, case studies to offer, skills to showcase, etc. Interviewing early in your career is the most daunting it will ever be.

The second thing you need to remember is this: interviews go both ways. Yes, you need a job, and you really want this one. However, the company also really needs an employee, and they really want you. If a company calls you in for an interview, that means they already like you and are excited about you! They saw your résumé and thought you'd be a great fit for the role. They want to talk to you further and see if you're a good fit for *each other.*

Unfortunately, though, some of us still suffer from interview anxiety, which often takes one of three different forms.

Some folks (like former me) experience physiological anxiety. Their mind knows they are a great fit for the job, but their body has other plans. If this is you, you have to regulate your nervous system. Avoid drinking coffee or energy drinks before the interview. You already have enough natural adrenaline running through your body – the last thing you need to add to that stew is caffeine and sugar. Also try moving around a lot. Go to a kickboxing class, or have a dance party in your living room. Imagine that adrenaline bouncing around inside your body, looking for a way out. The antidote is movement.

The second type of preinterview anxiety is mental anxiety. This anxiety stems from a feeling of not being qualified for the role. This anxiety says things like, *They're going to laugh at you,* or *You're just wasting your time,* or *Everyone else they're interviewing is better than you.* These thoughts bounce around in your head, shredding your confidence.

I can't stress this enough: If you are in a job interview, you 100 per cent belong and deserve to be there. If you didn't, you wouldn't have been invited. No one would waste their time bringing you in for an interview if they didn't think you could be a good fit for the role. That would be silly.

One thing that helps with mental anxiety is preparation. Use your nervous energy for good! Research the company, study their competitors, listen to a podcast interviewing the CEO, etc. Also practise. Ask a friend to do a mock interview with you and give you feedback on your answers.

Or throw the job description and your résumé details into a generative AI program like ChatGPT and ask, 'Based on this information, can you give me three reasons why I am the perfect candidate for this role?' Focus on positive affirmations like, 'I'm a great fit for this role! I have all these skills and qualifications that they're looking for. I'm a great person to work with, and an interview is just a meeting.'

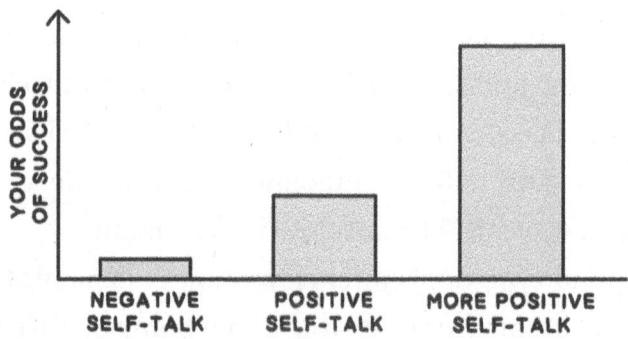

The third and final root cause of preinterview anxiety goes a bit deeper, and you might not even know if you have it. This type of anxiety stems from a lack of self-esteem. You may seem cool, calm and collected before an interview, but your mind is racing. Deep down, you feel like you're just not good enough.

The fix for this unfortunately isn't as easy as a dance party or a reframing technique. This type of anxiety requires deep work, and you have to want to do it and believe you are worthy of something better. You are the author of your own life, writing a new page every day. No one else has access to your pen and paper.

In his book *The Four Agreements*, Don Miguel Ruiz writes, 'Maybe we cannot escape from the destiny of the human, but we have a choice: to suffer our destiny or to enjoy our destiny.' The first step here is a radical act of self-love: deciding that you deserve a good life. You can then take steps from there, which may include finding a good therapist, daily journalling, embracing healthy habits, etc. Brick by brick, you can rebuild your self-esteem and become the best version of yourself in and outside of interviews.

Top Five Tips for Nailing Your Interview

I want you to walk into every interview feeling fully prepared, polished and ready to shine. Before we dive into the scripts, here are my top five, five-star, can't-fail tips for absolutely nailing your interview.

1. LOOK GOOD

I know this sounds weird, but science doesn't lie. This has been researched over and over throughout the years, and the truth is that people like and trust attractive people. If someone is conventionally attractive, we tend to assume that they are trustworthy, responsible and capable. Yes, it's entirely unfair. Don't even get me started! But it's also something that all humans are guilty of. It's a subconscious bias that many of us don't even realize we're acting on in the moment. This is one reason it is so important for anyone conducting job interviews to go through unconscious bias training – but that's a rant for another time.

The good news is that, to an extent, you can control what you look like. I implore you: Take a shower, brush your teeth, do your hair, put on makeup if that's your thing, iron your clothes, use deodorant (probably more than usual – let's be honest), and skip the cologne or perfume, as it gives people headaches. Look put together, and people will assume you are as put together as you look.

When it comes to what to wear in a job interview, I have one constitutional law of the land: You cannot be overdressed; you can only be underdressed. Always err on the side of being overdressed.

More specifically, there's an unwritten rule that in an interview you should dress one step up (in terms of formality) from how employees at the company typically dress. Obviously, the pandemic ruined this, because now a ton of people work from home in their pyjamas (and I don't blame them). But if the company wears 'smart casual', which is something like jeans and a nice shirt (think tech bros in Silicon Valley), you would wear one step up from that, which is business casual (think Meghan Markle in *Suits*). For women, business casual is nice slacks or a skirt, a blouse with maybe a blazer on top, and flats or heels.

For men, business casual is slacks, a button-down shirt, and oxfords or loafers.

If the office is business casual, you would dress one step up from that, which is business formal. This is basically a suit and formal shoes (heels, loafers or pumps). If you'd rather wear a dress, it should be a professional, conservative dress. And if they wear business formal at the company, then you should absolutely show up in a tux or an evening gown. Just kidding! If they're business formal, you can just wear business formal. That's where the buck stops.

If you have no idea what the people working at this company wear because you don't work there yet (duh), go to the company's Instagram page or website and look at what people are wearing in the photos. Remember, you can't be overdressed! Okay, unless you're wearing a tuxedo to an interview at McDonald's, but honestly, they would probably just get a kick out of that and bring you on as a personality hire, so . . .

2. PRACTISE, PRACTISE, PRACTISE

I promise you that the more you practise for your job interview, the easier it's going to be and the more articulate you are going to sound. If you can, practise with a friend or colleague who is willing to roast you. Don't ask your mum. She's just going to tell you, 'That was great, sweetie!' No. Ask someone that you know will give you honest feedback and help you see any blind spots. (I mean, that could be your mum. I don't know your mum. So, up to you.)

Another massively effective trick to instantly improving your interview skills is to record yourself. I know, it can be super uncomfortable to watch yourself on video. Trust me, I do it every day, and it never gets easier. With that said, it's extremely effective for seeing yourself how others see you.

When practising, pay attention to your tone, body language and speed. It's important to speak low, slow and down. When we get anxious, we tend to speed up, speak in a higher pitch and go up at the end of our sentences? Like everything is a question? And we're unsure of ourselves? Slow down, speak in your natural register and complete your sentences definitively.

And finally, don't be afraid to pause. The interviewer isn't going anywhere. Showing that you can take a beat to think, collect your thoughts and embrace the silence shows professionalism and poise.

3. MAKE IT ABOUT THEM

So many people go into a job interview thinking about themselves, but interviewers don't want to hear that you're looking for a new job that pays better or where you can have a nicer boss. They don't want to hear that this would be a strategic career move for you or a good way to transition into another industry. They only want to hear about how your skills are going to bring value to their company.

At the end of the day, the key to job interviews is simple: Tell the company what they want to hear. How do you figure out what they want to hear? You don't have to speculate or play games – use that job description as your outline.

Did the job description say they want someone who is collaborative? Then say that you're collaborative! Did it say that they're looking for someone who is a team player, self-motivated and resourceful? Wow, what a coincidence! You are a resourceful team player who is self-motivated!

For example, if they ask, 'Why do you want to work here?' you could say, 'It would look really good on my résumé, as I'm trying to transition from health care into tech.' Yes, that's truthful. But it does nothing for the interviewer.

Instead, try something like, 'I'm very interested in this position because I'm passionate about leveraging technology to better our health-care system. As a health-care administrator for five years, I witnessed firsthand how much opportunity there is for innovation in hospital technology. I'm eager to utilize my skills and expertise to help successfully bring Health Tech's latest products to the market. I'm confident that my background in project management, programme coordination, and systems implementation combined with my innate passion for bettering our health-care system makes me a fantastic fit for this role.'

Well, well, well. I think we have a winner.

4. KEEP IT POSITIVE

I've said it before and I'll say it again: There is one thing that will automatically make you sound more professional, and that is a positive attitude. I don't care if your last boss was the love child of Passive-Aggressive Patricia and Micromanaging Mike. Avoid saying anything negative in an interview about anyone or anything. Instead, use positive language that is affirmative and empowering.

For example, if an interviewer tells you about a current challenge the department is facing, instead of saying, 'Yeah, that sounds like a problem for sure,' or 'That sounds really annoying,' instead try, 'If hired, I would be more than happy to assist with that,' or 'That sounds like a really exciting challenge,' or 'I know a great software that might make that process easier.'

Being positive also means being a yes man or a yes woman. For instance, if they ask if you're interested in other tasks outside the job description, don't shut it down right away. They're just gauging, and you're not making a commitment. You can always say something neutral like, 'I'd definitely be interested in learning more about that.' We're going to talk more about specifics of what to say in job interviews later on, but for now, just remember the three P's: positive, professional and poised.

5. SPEAK WITH YOUR BODY

Earlier, you read about why body language is so important and how to communicate professionally through body language. This is more important than ever in a job interview. If you're

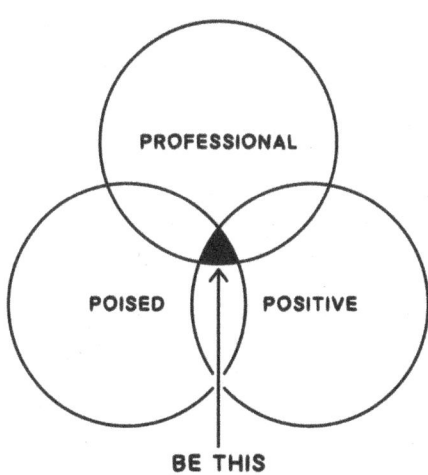

nervous, you might slouch, cross your arms, fidget, rock back and forth, or bounce your leg up and down. You might not even realize how your nerves are showing up physically. This is another good thing to look out for when watching a video of yourself.

It might feel awkward to you at first, but in a job interview, you want to sit up straight and slightly forward. Roll your shoulders back and down. Pretend there is a string from the top of your head pulling you up to the ceiling. Feel free to cross your legs or keep both feet planted on the ground, and keep your hands visible – out of your pockets and ideally placed on your lap or on the table. Don't fidget!

Again, dancing, moving, running and meditating beforehand can help you be more relaxed and still in your body. Take deep breaths. Box breathing is an incredibly helpful technique for regulating your nervous system when you're anxious. It goes like this: Breathe in for four seconds, hold your breath for four seconds, breathe out for four seconds, hold your breath for four seconds, and repeat. This naturally communicates to your body and mind, 'We got this.'

The Four Types of Interview Questions

By now, hopefully you're feeling pretty good walking into your interview. But there's one other small thing we have to cover: what you're actually going to say! There are specific things you should say and things you should never say in an interview. So buckle up, because you are about to learn exactly how to make yourself sound as amazing in interviews as you really are.

Interview questions typically fall into one of four categories: basic questions, behavioural questions, technical questions, and outlier questions. Here are the most common questions in each of these categories, along with tips and scripts to help you answer each one with ease. While the exact wording may vary, most of these questions are fairly predictable. So if you go into your interview prepared to answer them, you can adapt your answers on the spot for pretty much anything they may throw at you.

BASIC INTERVIEW QUESTIONS

'Tell me about yourself.'

Why is it that whenever an interviewer says, 'Tell me about yourself,' I suddenly forget everything about who I am, where I came from, and what I'm doing there? Sometimes, the simplest questions are the hardest to answer because they're just so broad. I mean, how do you summarize the entirety of your life into a 120-second answer?

Well, have no fear, my friend. I have a simple formula that will help you nail this question in any context for the rest of your life. It goes like this: past, present, future. That's it! Tell them a little about your background – where you've worked, your degrees, certifications and maybe where you grew up (but this isn't necessary). Then, focus on your present. Tell them about what you're currently doing and what you've recently achieved (remember to keep it positive!). Finally, talk a little about your future aspirations.

For example, don't say something like:

'Well, for starters, I'm a Virgo rising INFJ ADHD 3w4 pescatarian. I'm really interested in actually making it in the film industry and eventually directing my own films. I'm looking for a job that's really stable where I can explore a lot of different projects and see which one works best for me but also has a good work-life balance.'

Instead, try:

First, start with the past: 'I'm originally from Columbia, Maryland, and I graduated from NYU Tisch in 2021 with a major in film and a minor in media and communications.'

Then, shift to the present: 'After graduating with a few internships, I decided to stay in New York City, and now I work as an acquisitions manager for HBO, which I love.'

Lastly, shift to the future. 'I'm looking to pivot to more of a boutique agency, where I can have a smaller team and work with more creative freedom.'

'Walk me through your résumé.'
This is sort of an annoying question because your résumé is likely sitting right in front of them, and you wish you could just say, 'Uh, but did you even read my résumé?' But don't do that. Suppress any annoyance and use this opportunity to highlight your skills and experience. However, don't literally walk them through your résumé: 'Well, at the top of my résumé you'll see my name, my address, the link to my LinkedIn profile...'

Instead, tell a little story in the chronological order of your résumé. Start with where you went to school and all the jobs you've had since then: 'As you can see, I went to the University of Maryland for marketing, and I was heavily involved in campus activities like student government and volunteering. I had a couple of internships at marketing agencies. After school, I accepted a full-time position at a marketing agency, where I focused on data analytics. I've been there for about two years. I also listed some of the types of software I'm familiar with, like Tableau, MATLAB and Metabase. Oh, and I'm fluent in Spanish.'

'Why do you want to work here?'
I know you want to just say, 'Oh, that one's easy: money!' But the interviewer would probably just write you off and spend the

rest of the interview thinking about what they're going to order for lunch. *Chipotle, maybe? Oh, but I had Mexican last night. . . . Maybe I'll ask Alex if she wants to check out the new poke bowl place with me.*

The trick here is to focus less on the 'why' and more on the 'here'. Obviously, you want a job for the money, but they're not asking why you want a job. They're asking why you want to work *here*. Why are you applying to this company over another? What piqued your interest? Start by homing in on elements of the company you like, and align those with your values and unique offering.

For example, if you liked the company mission, then start there:

'I admire this company for so many reasons, especially your commitment to showcasing work that other studios tend to overlook.'

Now, connect it to your mission: 'I've always been passionate about independent film and discovering what's next.'

Then it's time for some flattery: 'And clearly, ABC Studios is the leader in independent film. I don't know how you hit the nail on the head with every release, but I want to be a part of your next hit. I believe my personal passion for indie film combined with my technical and creative capabilities and experience make me the perfect candidate for the role.'

'Why should we hire you?'

This is your opportunity to humble brag like there's no tomorrow. Just kidding! Well, kind of. But what the interviewer is actually saying here is, 'Make your case to me, so I can make your case to my boss.'

It's always important to remember that 90 per cent of the time in a first interview, the person interviewing you isn't going to be the one who decides to hire you. So the priority needs to be making the case to them so they can make it to someone else. I recommend covering three things in your answer: your *hard skills* (ability to handle technical aspects of the job), your *soft skills* (personality, character and interpersonal strengths), and your *unique offering* (what you bring to the table that no one else does). This is a way to spin past experience (that's maybe not super relevant) as a strength. For example:

'I think I'd be a great fit for this role for a few reasons. First, I have the hard skills you're looking for. I have experience in several project management systems and new AIs, and I continuously self-educate on the latest programs to keep up with the industry. I also have strong communication and interpersonal skills. I'm organized, proactive, collaborative, and I love working with a team to make sure we're on schedule and on budget. But what makes me unique is that I know your clients because I used to sit on that side of the table. In my previous role, I was the one communicating with agencies. So I have the unique ability to empathize with clients and understand them to make sure they feel in the loop and happy with our work.'

Now, what if you get asked the same question, but you don't have any experience? First of all, don't focus on your inexperience! This signals a lack of value and confidence. You can signal your value regardless of experience by focusing on your passion and skills.

Don't say, 'To be honest, I didn't go to college for this or any-

thing, and I don't have any previous experience, but I'm super down to learn!'

Try this instead: 'I noticed in the company's mission statement you talk about pushing boundaries and breaking the rules. One of my biggest professional fears is creating uninspiring, unoriginal and mediocre work. Pushing boundaries is second nature to me. I'm also a rule breaker when it comes to traditional education. Instead of going to a traditional art school, I opted to earn a Google UI/UX Design Certificate and completed the General Assembly 10-week UX/UI Design Bootcamp, meaning that I'm familiar with all the latest design practices. So, if I'm hired, you can rest assured that I will keep pushing myself and others to continue creating the original work that this company already does so well.'

'What is your greatest strength?'

When someone asks about your greatest strength in an interview, they aren't looking to hear you brag about how you can cook the perfect steak or something generic like 'I'm a hard worker.' What they're looking to see is how you speak positively about yourself. Are you confident? Are you self-aware? How is your ego?

My secret sauce for answering this question is to say a desirable strength of yours (bonus points if it aligns with the job description) but disguise it as a compliment you've received from someone else.

For example, instead of saying, 'I'm a hard worker,' try something like this:

'I've had previous managers tell me that I'm really dependable. They can always count on me to get the job done right and on time. It means a lot to me when I hear that. I value integrity and being someone you can trust with important tasks.'

'What is your greatest weakness?'

Ah, one of my absolute favourite interview questions: 'So, can you tell me something you suck at?' But really, this question is tricky because they're not actually asking you to tell them about how you hit snooze on your alarm seventeen times or eat the whole pint of Ben & Jerry's in one sitting. What they're really getting at is this: What are your red flags? How self-aware are you? Do you work to improve yourself? How do you speak critically of yourself?

I have a secret formula for answering this question: the 90/10 Rule. Spend 10 per cent of your answer naming the weakness and 90 per cent of your answer elaborating on how you're working to improve it. Another golden tip? Don't say, 'My weakness is . . .' Instead, try: 'Something I'm actively working to improve . . .' or 'Right now, I'm challenging myself to be . . .'

For example, 'Right now, I'm challenging myself to be a better listener. I've noticed that sometimes I get in my head when other people are talking. I'm currently reading a book on how to improve my active-listening skills, and I have to say it's really helping.'

Or: 'I hate to admit it, but I'm bad at remembering names. I've been using a tip I learned on a podcast where I repeat the person's name when I meet them. You might have noticed that today when we met, I repeated your name. It really works!'

Or: 'One thing I'm working on is my delegation skills. Sometimes I think it's easier to just do everything myself, but I know that to grow into more senior roles, I need to master this skill. I'm currently challenging myself to delegate at least one task a week, no matter how big or small.'

Oh, and one more thing: Do not say that you're a perfectionist. That will 100 per cent lead to some major eye rolling. You can say, 'I have trouble letting go of projects,' or 'Sometimes I get too in the weeds on the details,' but don't label yourself with your weakness. Saying 'I'm a perfectionist' is like saying 'I am a chronic liar,' or 'I am just a really loud person.' It implies rigidity, like you can't be changed and your weakness is part of your character and identity. Make the weakness separate from you and something you're actively working to eliminate.

'Why are you leaving your current job?'
(Or 'Why did you leave your last job?')
Stop, wait! Before you answer this question by saying, 'Oh, well, my boss was a psychopath,' keep in mind that they don't actu-

ally care why you left your last job. They're looking for red flags and trying to understand why you might leave *this* job. So don't answer this directly. You have to be professional and a little bit delicate with your answer. Of course, your exact answer will depend on what actually happened. For example:

If you were fired or laid off:

Don't: 'I got fired. Or laid off or whatever. Yeah, it really sucked.'

Do: 'Unfortunately, I was affected by massive restructuring, and nearly my entire team was let go. It was hard for me because I really enjoyed my work and my team, but ultimately I'm grateful because it allowed me to pursue this role.'

If you had or have a toxic boss:

Don't: 'Oh, my boss is literally insane.'

Do: 'Over the past year or so, there has been a shift in the management style, which has led me to pursue other opportunities. It was unfortunate because I've enjoyed the projects I've worked on, but it feels like the right time to move on.'

If you wanted a salary increase:

Don't: 'I kept asking for a raise, and they wouldn't give me one.'

Do: 'I've really enjoyed my time there and I'm proud of the skill set I developed and the team I led. But I'm ready for my next challenge and to take on a more senior position.'

'What are your salary expectations?'

Okay, so we are going to do a whole chapter together on negotiating during a job interview, but here's what I need you to know right now: This question is where the negotiation begins. Here are some things you should absolutely not say, right off the bat:

'Well, I currently make sixty-five thousand dollars, so anything more than that would be awesome!' Never, ever tell them your current salary. In fact, in several US states, it is against the law for them to ask about your salary history. Just because you're underpaid now shouldn't mean you'll keep being underpaid forever!

'I was hoping to make like around sixty-six thousand dollars? But I can go lower if I need to.' Never say what you're hoping to make. Never put out one single number.

'I don't really know!' It might seem like you'd make them happy by saying you don't know or care, but it actually does the exact opposite. Pretending like you're apathetic about how much money you make shows a lack of confidence, professionalism, and drive.

Now, what do you say? My advice is to politely ask for their salary range. Every single company has an approved budget for the role. Trust me, before creating a job posting, they have to get budget approval for that role. This might be a range or salary band – all you need to do is ask for it. And remember to save the actual negotiating for after you get the offer!

For example: 'Thank you so much for bringing that up. I definitely want to make sure we're aligned before moving forward. Do you know the approved salary range for the position?'

If they say something like, 'We don't have a set range. It depends on the candidate,' you can reply with, 'I'd like to learn more about the specifics of the role before giving out a solid number, but I can tell you my salary is flexible depending on other elements of the compensation package.'

If they won't let up, you can give them a range. For example: 'I'm currently interviewing for roles in the sixty- to ninety-thousand-dollar range. But, as I mentioned, I'm flexible on salary depending on other elements of the compensation package.'

'Where do you see yourself in five years?'
It can be tough to answer this. I mean, who knows what the state of the world will be in five years? Will there still be a thing called jobs?

Luckily, you don't have to be able to predict the future to answer this one. Just mention your current goals, how they're aligned with the company's goals, and then talk about your long-term eventual goals, even if they're not exactly set in stone.

For example: 'Right now, I'm looking to gain more experience in feature production and truly gain a mastery of all the different facets of large-budget production from beginning to end. That's why this position is so appealing to me. I can apply my studio and animation knowledge to larger-budget films.

Eventually, my goal is to be a lead producer who is well-rounded and can successfully bring these large projects to life.'

'Can you tell me about this gap on your résumé?'
No, you can't say you signed an NDA (unless of course, you actually did sign an NDA). But seriously, don't panic if you took some time off work for any reason and assume no one will ever hire you again. Companies tend to be much more lenient about this than they used to be.

Taking some time off doesn't make you any less qualified. Again, apply the 90/10 Rule. Spend only 10 per cent of your answer actually explaining the gap, and 90 per cent of the time talking about your competency, knowledge and improved skills. And remember, if you did any work on the side during your time off, then you were a freelancer! You were self-employed! Lean into that entrepreneurial energy.

Again, your exact answer will depend on the situation. For example:

> **Don't:** 'My grandma got really sick and no one else would step up to take care of her, so I had to quit my job and move in with her.'
>
> **Do:** 'I had to temporarily step back to care for a sick relative, but it's resolved now, and I'm so excited to dive right back into full-time work. While I wasn't working full time, I did freelance a bit and made sure to keep up with all new software developments.'

Don't: 'Oh, I was just a stay-at-home mum. Nothing but nappies and cartoons for three years! Bluey is pretty cool though.'

Do: 'I made the lifestyle decision to spend time raising my young children. During that time, in addition to being a full-time caretaker, I attended workshops, conferences, and stayed up to date on industry trends and news. Now that the kids are in school, I'm so excited to dive back into the industry. It truly feels like I haven't missed a beat.'

Don't: 'Ummm . . . that's personal.'

Do: 'Due to personal matters, I had to temporarily step back from full-time work. I'm happy to say that everything has been resolved, and I'm so excited to dive back in.'

'Are you interviewing at other companies?'

This question is essentially the same as a third date asking, 'So, are you dating other people, or . . .?' If you say no, it might signal that you aren't taking your job search seriously. If you say yes, it may signal that you don't actually want this job – you just want any job. So you have to be delicate with your approach.

Reiterate that you really do want this job, but you're also an in-demand professional. People have a natural aversion to loss. So as long as you strike the right tone, this answer can work in your favour. For example:

Don't: 'Yeah, I actually had another interview just this morning!'

Do: 'While I am particularly interested in this role and think it's a fantastic fit, I am exploring other opportunities at similar companies. To be completely transparent with you, though, this role is my number one pick and priority.'

HOW TO ANSWER ILLEGAL/INAPPROPRIATE QUESTIONS

Sometimes you get asked a question in an interview and think, 'Wait, I do not want to answer that. Do I have to??' If the question doesn't directly relate to the job, you don't have to answer. But of course, refusing to answer a question in an interview might feel awkward. Don't worry – I have you covered.

You should know that according to current UK laws and employment policies, there are certain questions that interviewers aren't supposed to ask, so any trained interviewer knows not to touch these questions with a ten-foot pole. Customs vary from country to country. In some countries, you're expected to include your marital status, race, and/or a picture on your résumé!

Most of the time, if you're in the UK and someone asks you one of these questions, they're just trying to make small talk and don't even realize they're asking something inappropriate. Here's how to politely evade the question and keep the interview moving along. And if you get the vibe that this person is asking in a malicious tone, feel free to end the interview, document what happened right afterwards, and report to the Equality and Human Rights Commission (EHRC).

If they ask anything like:

'It looks like you're married – do you have any kids?'

'Do you live with your husband, boyfriend, partner . . . ?'

'This job has pretty long hours. Do you mind telling me if you're married?'

'Do you have any disabilities I should know about?'

You can try:

'I'm sorry, I didn't get that, can you repeat the question?'

'Oh, will my answer to that question impact my chances of getting this job?'

'You don't have to worry about me. I'm prepared to do this job well.'

> Of course, it all depends on the context and tone. Asking them if your answer will impact your chances of getting the job may come off intimidating and litigious if you use the wrong tone. And if their question was just an innocent attempt at small talk, that can be unfortunate for both parties. It's best to give the benefit of the doubt first, and then if you suspect discrimination is at play, document and report to the EHRC.

BEHAVIOURAL QUESTIONS

Behavioural questions are essentially just story times. These questions usually start with, 'Tell me about a time when...' and are a chance to share anecdotes that perfectly illustrate what a valuable, professional hire you would be. It's super important to prepare a few specific stories ahead of time, usually centring around a time you dealt with an obstacle and overcame it, and keep those in your back pocket so you're not racking your brain in the moment.

While you won't know exactly which behavioural questions you'll be asked, you can probably adapt your stories to fit slightly different questions. In general, you want to have a story for the following scenarios:

1. A time you showed leadership
2. A time you adapted to a new situation
3. A time you handled conflict
4. A time you made a mistake

To frame these stories, I like to use the acronym STAR: 'Situation, Task, Action, Result'. Set the scene (situation), what you needed to do (task), how you stepped up (action), and what happened in the end (result). Here are some of the most common behavioural questions and scripts for how to best answer them.

'Tell me about a time you failed.'
I really, really hate this question. Why are they making you talk bad about yourself? Don't take the bait and actually disrespect yourself ('I'm honestly such a scatterbrain sometimes'), and don't get defensive ('In my last job I got blamed for losing this huge account, but it wasn't my fault!').

The key here is to take ownership of the 'failure' and talk about how you learned from it. Again, my 90/10 Rule comes into play! Aim to spend 10 per cent of the time talking about the mistake and 90 per cent of the time talking about what you learned, how you fixed it, and how you've grown.

For example: 'In my previous role, I was in charge of a project that had a tight deadline and a ton of moving parts. As the project manager, I was tasked with client communication, and I made the mistake of overpromising to please the client. This led to the client being understandably irritated when I had to tell them we were behind schedule, and this led them not to renew their contract with the company. I take full ownership of my mistakes, and I used what I learned to become a better project manager. I now know that being up front and honest with clients is key to building trust and creating long-term relationships.'

'Tell me about a time you disagreed with your boss or your coworker.'

Trust me, the interviewer is not asking for a juicy gossip session with all the tea. Now, I would love to hear it (email me the drama later), but the interviewer? Nope. They're asking about how you handle conflict and want to hear a carefully crafted story about when you acted professionally and asserted yourself.

This is your opportunity to showcase your poise and maturity. The trick here is to stress that you prioritized the company over anything else. So your story shouldn't be about a personal disagreement. Instead, talk about a time when your boss or coworker wanted to do something that you felt wasn't in the company's best interest.

For example: 'I do actually have a story that comes to mind. My team was working on a project where the client wanted to reference a specific TikTok trend. Everyone on the team, including my manager, was on board, but I had a gut feeling that it was inappropriate for this client and might lead to backlash online. Although I was just a junior account manager, I immediately raised the concern to my manager because it was in the best interest of the client and the company. Once I pointed it out, she agreed and got on the phone with the client. We were able to pivot the campaign, and it ended up being a success.'

'Tell me about a time when you demonstrated leadership.'

Don't shy away from this question, even if you have never managed another person or led a project in your life. Don't you dare say something like, 'Oh, I prefer to stick in the background . . .' They really just want to hear about a time when you stepped up to the plate or acted in any sort of proactive way. It doesn't have to be about leading the charge into battle.

You can focus on something big or small using the following formula: First, define what leadership means to you. Then, tell the story. Finally, wrap up with how it felt to step up and lead.

For example:

'To me, leadership is the ability to be a good listener and make decisions. In my previous role, there was a time when we were gearing up to launch a new product. The team had been working hard for months, and then one week before the launch, the team leader got into a car accident. He's okay, but he was in the hospital for two weeks, and management asked if I could step in to lead the project. I listened to my colleagues and developed an action plan. Turns out, the launch was a big success, and management was thrilled that we were able to rally. To be honest, it felt really good to be a leader and to make those kinds of game-time decisions. I work well under pressure, and I feel very fortunate that I had such great colleagues to lean on.'

TECHNICAL QUESTIONS

You may or may not be asked these, depending on the type of job you're applying for – they're about the hard, technical skills needed for the job. But be prepared just in case! These are basically a chance to show that you talk the talk and walk the walk and possess the hard skills necessary for the job.

'How would you approach editing a video (or another relevant task)?'

Hot tip – this is a chance to talk about your workflow, so don't say, 'Umm . . . I'd just . . . do it.' They want to see how you think through and tackle a complex task. To make it simple, break it down into your first, second, and third steps.

It's also a good idea here to ask questions back and get some clarification. Turn it into more of a conversation. This can show that you're familiar with the territory and know how to think things through. Maybe you want to ask, 'Who would I be collaborating with?' or 'Would I be working with any outside agencies?' Once you have all the information, go through your steps and top it off with, 'That's how I would do it, but I'm open to learning if there are other processes that this company finds more efficient.'

For example:

> **Start broad:** 'First, I would get my bearings on the project. I'd get all my assets organized on my hard drive and in bins, read the brief, and import all the footage.'

Next, get more in the weeds: 'Then I would storyboard according to the client script, and cut together a rough sequence for pacing. I would also find the music and SFX at this stage.'

Finally, wrap it up: 'After a few rounds of internal and external revisions, I'd picture lock, put the final touches on sound and colour, and make sure all the licences are cleared for usage. I'm open to learning if there are other processes that this company finds more efficient!'

'Are you familiar with this software?'

Although this is technically a closed question, never answer it – or any other interview question – with a simple, 'Yeah, of course,' or 'Nope, never heard of it.' In the world of improv, there is a credo called, 'Yes, and…' This means that you always expand on the other performer's line of thinking. Do that here by expanding on your answer and really speaking to your expertise.

For example, if the answer is yes: 'Yes! I am very familiar with that software. I used it every day at my previous job.'

If the answer is no, try spinning it positively: 'Yes, I am familiar with it, but I typically use another software. I'll put in the extra work to get up to speed on the latest updates and features.' Remember, everything is figure-out-able!

OUTLIER QUESTIONS

And finally, we arrive at the outlier questions. These are curveball questions that seem super random, as if they were designed to throw you off your game. For instance, Google famously used to ask people, 'Why are manholes round?' Microsoft asked, 'How would you test an elevator?' Apple asked, 'If you were a pizza delivery person, how would you benefit from scissors?' And Trader Joe's asked, 'What do you think about garden gnomes?'

These questions may seem really odd (and they are), but they are just a chance for the interviewer to see how you think under pressure and how you might approach a challenge. The trick here is to stay calm. Don't just say, 'I don't know.' These questions are usually sort of silly, so feel free to have fun with them and show off your personality. Ask questions back, like, 'How big are the scissors?' or 'Are the garden gnomes alive?' Then just answer in a way that isn't necessarily definitive but shows that you thought the question through in an intelligent way.

How to Ask the Right Questions in an Interview

At the end of every interview, the interviewer will almost always ask, 'Do you have any questions for me?' Answering no to this question is the only wrong answer. It signals a lack of preparation and genuine interest in the role. Remember, interviews are a two-way street. Having thoughtful questions prepared demonstrates your engagement, curiosity, and professionalism – qualities every interviewer values. So don't miss this chance to make a strong impression and show how invested you are in the opportunity.

The best questions for you to ask at the end of an interview fall into one of two categories: questions that make you look good and questions that actually help you gain information about the company. Sure, some questions might serve both purposes, but not always.

Here are examples of some of the best questions to ask that will help you look good:

- **Recent news:** I saw that a new disclosure rule was recently enacted. How do you think this will affect business?
- **Onboarding:** What is the onboarding process like for new employees, and what can I expect to be working on in my first ninety days?
- **Goals:** What would you say is the number one goal for the department over the next months?
- **Favourite day:** Personally speaking, what has your favourite day on the job been so far and why?
- **Values/culture:** I saw on the website that sustainability is a top priority for the company. Can you share a little bit about how that's implemented?

And here are some tactful questions that will give you more insight into what it's actually like to work for this company:

- **Instead of asking,** 'So, is this company toxic? Why did the last person up and leave?' Try: 'Are you able to share why this position is vacant?'
- **Instead of asking:** 'Do y'all give a lot of paid vacation days? Because I'm not trying to work at a company that only gives two weeks.' Try: 'My current company has a fixed twenty-five-day paid holiday rule – how does that compare here?'
- **Instead of asking:** 'Do you guys give bonuses or . . .' Try: 'How does the company celebrate and reward employees' successes?'
- **Instead of asking:** 'Is this company super political and bureaucratic? Cause if so, I'm out.' Try: 'How would you describe the organizational structure here, and which department makes major decisions?'
- **Instead of asking:** 'I'm trying to have a kid soon, is that gonna suck?' Try: 'I noticed on the website the company says it prioritizes family values. Can you tell me a bit more about that?'

And remember: When asking either type of question, practise active listening! This will ensure that you really understand what is being said while sounding professional and fully engaged in the conversation.

WOW, WE JUST got through some serious professional development jujitsu, and you did fantastic. Checking in here to make sure you're still with me, as I know this can all be a lot. But remember, interviewing is just a skill, like tennis, knitting or baking. It's not something anyone is born knowing how to do. We all have to learn it step-by-step. Now, take a break, go practise what you learned, and come back, because I have a lot (and I mean *a lot*) more to teach you!

CHAPTER 6

Negotiate Without Being Awkward

If you don't ask, the answer is always no.
—NORA ROBERTS

I admit that the title of this chapter is a bit misleading, because negotiating is inherently awkward for most people. (Sociopaths, you are exempt.) I always like to say that if you're going to try to negotiate and it doesn't feel at least a teeny-tiny bit awkward, you're probably doing it wrong. Good negotiating is not always comfy cosy, at least not at first. But if you can learn to live through ten seconds of awkward silence, you'll make exponentially more money throughout your life.

In his book *The 4-Hour Workweek*, Timothy Ferriss writes, 'A person's success in life can usually be measured by the number of uncomfortable conversations he or she is willing to have,' and I couldn't agree more.

For example, meet Kelsey, a somewhat anxious twenty-two-year-old graduate from the University of Maryland. She studied

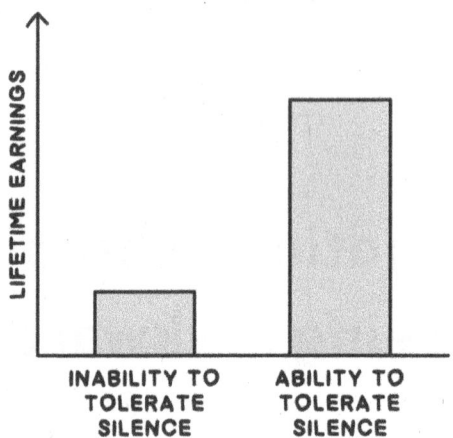

public health, graduated summa cum laude with four internships under her belt, and then started interviewing for entry-level jobs in Washington, DC. During the third Zoom interview for a job she really wants, she feels her face turn hot and her palms clam up as the interviewer asks her the dreaded question, 'What are your salary expectations?'

Kelsey fumbles, not knowing what the right answer might be, and just tries to say something that will make the interviewer happy. 'Oh, um, well, I just graduated, so this would be my first real salary,' she says. 'I mean, I obviously want to make a good salary, but whatever you're offering should be fine!'

The interviewer asks, 'So would around fifty thousand dollars a year work for you?'

Kelsey thinks to herself, *Fifty thousand dollars a year? In this economy? Living in D.C.?!* She knows that some of her friends have received offers well over this amount, and they didn't even intern throughout college. But Kelsey really wants the job, and talking about money makes her uncomfortable. She doesn't want to come off rude or ungrateful. So she says, 'Sure, that would be fine.'

The interviewer smiles and writes something down. Kelsey ends up getting the job, and indeed gets paid $50,000 a year. Many Americans make this much or less, but the cost of living in an expensive city like Washington, DC, combined with student loans, health-care costs and taxes, make it hard for Kelsey to make ends meet. She has to be very careful with her spending, live with several roommates, and cut out any 'fun' in her life.

Of course, most of us have to do this when we're just starting out. I certainly was not going on European vacations or eating at Michelin-starred restaurants when I was twenty-two, and I don't encourage you to expect that sort of lifestyle so early in your career either! However, what Kelsey doesn't know is that another recent graduate, Laura, is hired for the same role at the same company and locked in $55,000 a year – simply because she knows how to negotiate.

Here's the thing: Companies expect you to negotiate, and they even respect you more when you do it properly. In a free-market economy, companies will pretty much always make you the lowest offer they can without you laughing in their face and walking away. Laura knows this, but Kelsey does not. It's part of the hidden curriculum, and I'm going to teach you the secret skills you need to start negotiating without feeling awkward, rude or offensive, or fearing that you're going to lose an offer. You'll learn not only what to say in a negotiation, but also how to feel good saying it. You'll be shocked by how easy and, dare I say, fun (???) negotiating can actually be.

The Snowball Effect

People often ask me, 'Should I negotiate my first job offer?' and my answer is always a resounding 'Yes!' Negotiating early on in your career is crucial because it leads to a snowball effect.

Let's go back to Kelsey and Laura for a moment. Thanks to her negotiation skills, Laura starts her career at a $55,000 salary and Kelsey at $50,000. Not a huge deal, right? But that small pay difference snowballs over time, leading to a bigger pay difference between the two. Say they both stay at the same company for ten years and only get incremental 3 per cent pay bumps each year. After ten years of the same 3 per cent raise, Laura is now making $6,300 more than Kelsey every single year. And over those ten years since they started working, she's made over $57,000 more than Kelsey in total.

Think about what you could do with an extra $57,000! If we want to take this further, imagine that Laura had invested that extra $57,000. It would have grown even more, putting her way ahead of Kelsey in terms of financial stability – all because she chose to have a very normal and simple conversation during her offer ten years prior.

I'm not just relying on anecdotes here. Research by the American Association of University Women (AAUW) found that negotiating a higher starting salary can lead someone to earn hundreds of thousands more over the course of a career compared to someone who does not negotiate.[5] Research from Carnegie Mellon University showed that individuals who negotiate their first job offer can earn up to $1 million more over their career than those who didn't.[6] Forget $57,000 – what would you do with an extra $1 million!?

In addition to the obvious monetary benefits, the emotional impact of negotiating early may be even more striking. Attempting to do something 'scary' and achieving it successfully is like your brain completing a marathon. Neurons connect in a new way to say, 'Oh, this is something new that we can do!' Your soul feels empowered, and your mental strength is fortified. Again, the proof is in the pudding – don't just take my word for it. A study from Harvard Business School shows that successfully negotiating leads to a boost in self-esteem and confidence, which in turn leads to increased job satisfaction and motivation.[7]

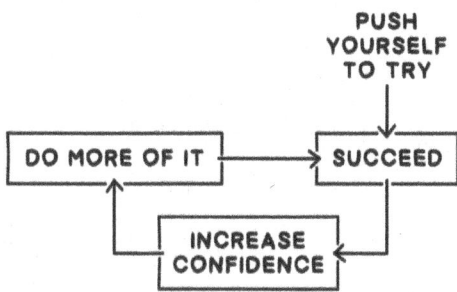

According to the Pew Research Center, only 30 per cent of Americans negotiated their last job offer.[8] However, of those 30 per cent who did, 85 per cent got some or all of what they asked for. So what the heck is stopping that other 70 per cent from negotiating? Well . . . fear. They're worried the offer will be rescinded or that they'll come off as ungrateful, rude, entitled, and/or difficult. Sure, 85 per cent of people negotiated successfully, but what about the other 15 per cent? Did they die?

No! In fact, they lived! If you try to negotiate, the absolute worst-case scenario is that the company says, 'Sorry, that's the highest we can go.' That's it. They say no, and you're still alive, the world is still spinning, and you still have the initial offer available. Even if that happens, you haven't failed. You can still work with them on nonsalary compensation like an increased employer pension contribution, more holiday days, flexible hours, a later start date, etc. More on this in a minute! Let's not get ahead of ourselves. I'm just so excited for you!

Maybe you're thinking, *No, Erin, the worst-case scenario is that they rescind the offer.* Listen to me: If a company takes back an offer simply because you asked them a question, trust me when I tell you that this is not a company you want to work for. A company getting offended by a professional custom is the biggest red flag there is. Companies that ghost people mid-offer are terrible companies, a waste of your time, and probably scamming people. That is that.

Now, if you've been out of work for a while and don't want to rock the boat on a fair offer, it is okay not to negotiate. Negotiating is always optional. However, a good employer will never rescind an offer after receiving a professional counteroffer. That does not happen.

When you're too scared to negotiate, another person is pulling it off successfully. High-calibre professionals negotiate, and it is what companies expect from desirable, highly skilled candidates. In fact, a study from the University of Iowa shows that negotiating can drastically increase your desirability and make the company gain respect for you.[9] Candidates who negotiate are seen as more confident and assertive.

If I haven't yet convinced you that you need to negotiate, let me say one more thing before I rest my case: You and a company have a transactional relationship. It's not personal; it's just professional. Remember that! One more time for the people in the back: It's not personal; it's just professional. Companies are paying you to do a job. You do the job, and they pay you. That's it. If you are providing value and they are underpaying you, that is not a good and balanced transaction. You are giving more than you're getting, and they are getting more than they're giving.

Start Negotiating Before Your Interview

Okay, are you ready to start negotiating? Contrary to popular belief, this process actually starts way before you begin throwing around numbers. Let me explain.

Even before your first interview, you need to start doing your research. Look at the market and the current economic status within your industry, and start gathering data on how much somebody in your area with your skill set is worth. Apologies in advance for how weird this is going to sound, but imagine that you are a product. If you were sitting on a shelf and a company was walking down the aisle looking at all the products, what would make you more valuable than the next one? Is it your degree? Your previous experience? Your technical skills? Your fantastic personality and positive attitude?

Figure out what your best qualities are and make sure there

is a corresponding salary amount. Charge more for your extra features! Not sure how to find out? Network! Talk to some friends in the industry and ask around to see what your skills are worth (and maybe learn some new skills). Then, craft your story to ensure you are this company's dream product.

A great way to gather information is through salary databases like checkasalary.co.uk, Payscale.com and Glassdoor.co.uk. All you have to do is spend some time lurking around the internet and come up with a range that you think is appropriate for your skill set, experience, and geography.

Data is your friend here for a few reasons. One, so you can be realistic about your expected salary. You know, don't throw out, 'I need one hundred thousand dollars,' just because you want to say that you 'make six figures'. Be realistic, and know your market value. You don't want to interview for a nonprofit job asking for tech industry numbers. It will make you look silly and unserious, and we don't want that!

Second, the more information you have, the better you will understand your leverage. Ah, here is where we talk about leverage, the be-all-end-all tool for how to succeed in business. To successfully negotiate, there are two things you need to be acutely aware of: your leverage and your audience.

KNOW YOUR LEVERAGE

Leverage comes from the word 'lever', which is a simple machine made of a beam and a fulcrum. When you push down on one side of the beam, the other side goes up. The more pressure or weight you can apply to your side, the more the other side will lift. This is leverage – the weight you can throw around in a negotiation.

In 1968, the New York City Department of Sanitation went on strike to demand wage increases, better working conditions, and recognition as vital city workers. These are the folks who manage and dispose of waste. When they decided to strike in February of that year, it only took nine days for the mayor to meet their demands. In those nine days of striking, one hundred thousand tons of garbage piled up on the streets of New York, sparking public outrage and a lot of stink.

The New York City sanitation workers of 1968 had something important: rock solid leverage. Them not working for even just a week caused such a disruption to the city that the mayor was forced to grant them what they wanted. Only when you have something the other party desperately needs can you have true leverage.

In your job search, you need to position yourself as someone who has leverage. You are a wonderful employee with a lot to offer, so would the company rather meet your demands or lose you to a competitor? Always enter into a negotiation knowing your leverage and what you have to offer that the company can't be without.

For example, if you currently have a job, but two other companies slide into your email and say, 'Come work for us! We'll pay you more and are totally better,' you now have a ton of leverage. You can go to your current employer and tell them about your situation in an effort to renegotiate your current salary. Of course, you want to tread lightly.

If you don't have a good relationship with your boss, are new to the company, and/or the company lays off employees frequently, I would avoid making it too obvious that you're considering leaving. However, if you have a solid relationship with your boss, have been a spectacular employee, and can have a candid conversation about pay, you can always try to use these counteroffers as leverage.

Finding the words for this conversation can be challenging, so here is some inspiration: 'Hi, boss, thanks for taking the time to meet with me. To be transparent with you, I've recently received two unsolicited offers that align with my market rate. However, I would prefer to keep working here, as I enjoy the work and my colleagues. Are you able to help me adjust my current compensation so I can stay?' Make sure they know that it's just about you doing what is best for you professionally. It's not personal, just professional.

I know you might be thinking, *Well, I don't have leverage. The company is interviewing a bunch of other people, they can pick anyone they want.* Wait, are you not interviewing at any other companies? Are you putting all your eggs in this one basket? I assume not! The last thing a company wants is to lose a high-quality candidate to one of their competitors.

Your leverage is the quality of your offering. That's why it's important to be really good at what you do and amazing to work with. Be a pleasant person, and know how to effectively articulate your unique offering.

If you're not sure what your unique offering is, talk to a friend, a mentor or a family member. Ask them, 'What do you think makes me uniquely qualified for this job?' This might sound crazy, but you can also try chatting with Gen AI. As a prompt, try something like, 'Pretend you're an expert career coach who's interviewing for X role at Y company in Z industry. My previous experience is ABC. What is my unique offering?' Then copy and paste the job description and your résumé.

Once you know your unique offering, remember that it is part of your leverage. For example, if a company needs someone who knows how to operate a specific software and you're one of the few available professionals with this skill, the company needs you more than you need them. Now you have options and leverage.

KNOW YOUR AUDIENCE

The second thing you need to be acutely aware of is your audience. Who are you talking to? What is their role? Do they have the power to actually give you what you want, or do they have to go make the case to someone else? Having this information will help you understand how to approach and communicate with this person.

For example, let's say you've been interviewing with Tara. Tara is a twenty-four-year-old recruiter at FinTech Company

(I don't know. I'm running out of fake company names. Just go with it.) Tara has a boss, a senior hiring manager, who has to coordinate with a department head and the finance department to green-light your counteroffer.

This means you want to make a case to Tara that she can then easily relay to her boss and their colleagues. Tara is a window, a portal, an ally, a collaborator. Don't try to argue with Tara. Instead, befriend Tara and find a way to make her excited about hiring you because it'll make her look really good to her boss.

However, let's say that you're interviewing for a small start-up, and the person interviewing you is the CEO. Since they don't need anyone else's approval to hire you, you just need to focus on convincing them. Don't get distracted by anything else; zero in on what that CEO wants and what he or she is looking for in a new hire.

Erin's Top Five Rules for Negotiating

When studying negotiation techniques, I often find that the most common advice is in one of two categories. First is the hypermasculine approach: 'Plant your feet in the ground and don't take no for an answer!' You strong-arm and essentially intimidate or psychologically manipulate your opponent into giving you what you want. The second approach is on the other side of the spectrum: 'Stand in your truth. Lead with authenticity.' I've always felt left out of these two approaches – the first one being too aggressive, and the second too squishy.

I'm here to teach you a new approach that's somewhere in

the middle and doesn't force you to change your personality or get a PhD in psychology in order to be a successful negotiator. Whether you are shy, extroverted, funny, serious, friendly, confident or modest, my negotiation methodology is going to meet you where you are. Successful negotiation is about being positive and collaborative. And if you aren't comfortable or confident with your strategy, it won't work. People don't like feeling manipulated or backed into a corner. So I'm going to teach you how to negotiate in a way that leaves everyone feeling great.

1. BE WARM

Social psychologist and author Amy Cuddy has researched the characteristics that people judge favourably in leaders and found that the two most important are warmth and competence. I have no doubt that you are already super competent. So make sure to add some warmth to your negotiations.

Warm folks are authentically kind, give you their undivided attention, appear relaxed and are humorous and inclusive. When negotiating, use a friendly tone, show empathy, be human and be kind. You're a reasonable person wanting to make a reasonable deal. Yes, negotiations are about getting someone else to give you what you want, and that is a delicate dance at times. But adding a little smile goes a long way to defuse tension and remind your counterpart that you're on the same team: Team Let's Get This Deal Done.

And no, warmth does not take away your power, not even a little bit. One of the best negotiators I've ever met is a sweet, polite, petite Midwestern woman. She will smile and nod and laugh at your unfunny jokes and say 'ruf' instead of 'roof' – it's adorable! Her affect is saying, 'I'm your friend, I'm sweet and I'm not intimidating at all!' Meanwhile, her words are dead serious, saying, 'If you don't find a way to make this work, I'm walking away forever.'

She is the opposite of intimidating, but she always gets what she wants by sweetly reiterating her needs and how badly she wants to make the deal work. She doesn't back down. She doesn't get embarrassed or sheepish. She makes what most people would think are ridiculous demands. But because she has a sweet smile plastered across her face, you never even realize you're dealing with a mastermind. You can say no a hundred times, and she'll respond with, 'Oh no! I'd really like to find a way to make this work,' a hundred and one times.

So next time you're in negotiation, swap out the 'Sixty K or I walk' with 'Oh, that's too bad. Are you sure we can't make this work? I would love nothing more than to sign this offer today, but I just can't do it for less than sixty-five thousand.' Remember the desired outcome for both parties: Get the contract signed.

2. DON'T OVEREXPLAIN

It's tempting to go into a negotiation wanting to defend the reasoning behind your needs. Your rent is going up, your wedding is next year, your student loans are due, and inflation is making everything more expensive. These reasons are all legit, but I'm going to tell you the truth: The company does not care. No offence, but none of these things will make them want to pay you more.

Remember, it's not personal; it's just professional. So it's much more effective to focus on your value in the market instead of your personal reasons for wanting more money. This is because it's a subtle threat that says, 'If you don't pay me X amount, your competitor will.' This is much more convincing than: 'Well, my student loans alone are like four hundred a month so . . .'

For example, let's say you're trying to ask for a raise at your current company. Don't say, 'Well, Miami is getting to be a really expensive city, I don't know how I'm going to be able to keep living on my own for sixty thousand, and I don't want to get roommates again! Can I please get a raise? Even just three thousand would work.'

Instead, try this: 'The market rate for a producer in Miami with my skill set and experience is seventy-three to eighty-one thousand dollars. And as you know, I'm currently being paid sixty thousand a year. Are you open to discussing an adjustment to my compensation to accurately align with my market value?' Mic drop.

3. STOP TRYING TO BE FAIR

A lot of negotiation experts talk about aiming for a 'fair deal', but I don't love the word 'fair'. It's a word that has a lot of emotion wrapped up in it. The problem with the word 'fair' is that it's entirely based on perception, and saying that something isn't 'fair' doesn't really make for a convincing argument. People don't agree to fair deals, they agree to deals they *feel* are fair.

When negotiating, facts are much more important than 'fair'. Making the case for your value is a much better argument than trying to get them to be fair.

So, instead of: 'I saw how much Sam is making, and it's five thousand dollars more than me, but she just started in June. That's not fair.'

Try this: 'I've recently been made aware that I'm being underpaid and would like to adjust my compensation to align with my market value. Are you open to discussing this?' Smile!

Again, your leverage is your choice and freedom. The market is paying more for people with your skill set. Don't make it about what's fair and who said who is getting paid whatever. Sure, you can use pay transparency as a tool, but limit that to an element of your argument instead of the cornerstone.

4. DON'T COME IN TOO HOT

Negotiations are about tact, craft and knowing when to step on the gas or put on the brakes. They are a back-and-forth. Again, you can't force someone to give you what you want. You need to make what you want into something they want. Don't come in too hot and demand what you need without any flexibility or grace.

Simply open up the conversation and consider their point of view. Maybe this company can't pay you any more, but they're offering flexible hours. That's great! They're working with you, so you need to work with them. Reiterate how excited you are and how much you want to sign the offer today. Recalibrate, modify, adjust and fine-tune your strategy with every response they give.

Let's say you're entering into a negotiation to ask your boss if you can switch to part-time work to save on daycare costs. Instead of: 'Hey, boss, I need to go part time. There's not enough work, and I know I can make an extra thousand bucks bartending.'

Try this: 'Hey, boss, how do you think things have been going lately? My workflow feels pretty light.'

Then listen to what they have to say. Maybe they respond with, 'Yes, sorry, losing our big client means we're in need of some new business.' Then you can take that information and reply, 'Would it be helpful if I went part time? I'm currently in a position where that's a possibility if you're open to it.' Again, keep your tone positive, collaborative and friendly. Are you asking them for something? Or are you giving them an opportunity to get something they want? (Hint: It's the latter!)

5. BE AN ALLY

Whenever you're negotiating a deal, it's important to remember that everyone wants to have a deal in place so they can move on with their lives. And no one wants this more than a recruiter. Recruiters' success is measured by how effectively, efficiently and successfully they staff a position. When a recruiter hires someone who ends up being a fantastic fit and brings a ton of value to the company, that is a pat on the back, two thumbs up, bonus material.

So when you're in a negotiation, always remember what the other party wants. Usually, it's to end the negotiation and reap the benefits of the deal. You are partners, not opponents. Be an ally, and remember that you have something they want. Don't rush the process. And don't let your need to please stifle your power.

For example, let's say you're in a negotiation and the company says they can't raise your salary any higher. Instead of: 'Well, if you can't match my salary request, I guess I have to say no, sorry.'

Try this: 'I'd love to sign this contract today and let you move on. I'm sure you're very busy. Any ideas on how we could make that happen if an increase in salary is off the table?'

Let's Negotiate: An Example Story

Okay, all that talk, talk, talk is exhausting, so let me walk you through a realistic example of a successful negotiation. Jessie is interviewing for a role as a software engineer at Fizzl, a hot new tech start-up. She currently works as a software engineer at another tech company and has all the hard skills needed for the role and a good amount of experience. So she feels confident in her leverage. She has also done her research and knows that the average salary for a software engineer in her city is $85,000 a year. The salary range is not listed in the job description, but she feels she is worth at least $90,000 a year.

During the first interview, the recruiter asks Jessie, 'What are your salary expectations?' Jessie is prepared and says, 'Thank you for bringing that up. I definitely want to make sure that we're aligned before moving forward. Do you know the approved salary range for this position?' The recruiter won't budge. She tells Jessie, 'We don't have a set range, I really need to just jot down a number.'

Jessie recalls a popular negotiation technique called mirroring. This is when you repeat the last few words or a phrase back to the person you're talking to. It's a good way to buy some time and get your opponent (I mean ally!) to elaborate and soften.

Jessie repeats the recruiter's words back to them. 'You don't have a set range?'

The recruiter replies, 'Yeah, the pay varies depending on skills and experience.'

In this scenario, Jessie has a 'walk-away' number of $90,000. Because of Jessie's leverage (currently being employed and not in a rush to find new work), she has the ability to walk away from an offer that doesn't meet her requirements. So Jessie reveals this, but in a tactful way:

'Got it, that makes sense. Well, I can tell you that I'm currently interviewing for positions in the ninety- to one-hundred-twenty-thousand-dollar range. But I can be flexible on salary depending on other elements of the compensation package.' Jessie smiles, striking the perfect tone. She gave a wide range with her desired number anchoring the base, all while reiterating her flexibility. Beautifully done.

This seems to appease the recruiter, who moves on and later calls Jessie back for two subsequent interviews before finally offering her the job. Jessie is thrilled at first, but that fades into disappointment when the official offer letter lists a yearly salary of $89,000 a year.

Jessie doesn't let this offer letter get her down, though, because she remembers what I taught her: The initial offer is often the lowest number a company thinks they can offer without you laughing and running away. This is the start of the negotiation.

So she responds, 'Thank you so much! I am so excited to join the team. However, the salary offered is a bit surprising to me, as I noted that ninety thousand dollars was my lowest expected salary during our initial interview. Due to my specialized skill set and the unique responsibilities of this role, I was expecting an offer closer to one hundred thousand dollars. Would you be able to help me get closer to that number?' Notice that she aims high, knowing that they would likely meet her somewhere in the middle.

Best-case scenario? The recruiter says, 'Absolutely understand. Let me see what I can do,' and then comes back with a $100,000 offer. Most likely scenario? The recruiter says, 'Absolutely understand. Let me see what I can do,' and then comes back with an offer somewhere in the middle. However, in the worst-case scenario, they say something like, 'I'm sorry, that's the highest we can go. We're a start-up, so we're working with a limited budget. There will be a lot of opportunities for growth though!'

This is what happens to Jessie. She's faced opposition at every stage of this journey, but she knows that with each obstacle comes opportunity.

'A lot of opportunities for growth?' Jessie mirrors.

'Yes, we're headed for a fundraising round with VCs, so hopefully everyone will get raises soon. It's not a guarantee, but a high probability.'

Jessie is curious and open. 'VCs, very nice. I'm curious, are there any other elements of the compensation package where we could make up for the lack of flexibility on salary?'

'We could offer stock, if you're interested,' the recruiter replies.

'I'd definitely be interested in learning more about that,' Jessie says. Notice that she doesn't say yes or no – just that she'd be interested in continuing the conversation.

The recruiter takes a day to gather a revised offer that includes stock in the budding start-up. Jessie is excited about the opportunity to work at Fizzl, so she says yes to an $89,000 base salary with eligibility for a performance bonus, a hybrid workspace, a flexible schedule, and an equity compensation plan. Considering all this, Jessie feels very satisfied with this offer.

(Note: This isn't necessarily a good offer for everyone, as stock in an early-stage start-up is a risky investment, but Jessie knows this industry well and is willing to take a calculated risk in exchange for the potential rewards.)

'Thank you so much for working with me on this,' Jessie replies. 'I would be happy to accept that offer.' Jessie reviews the offer to make sure their promises align with what is in writing, and starts her new job. Congrats, Jessie!

Negotiating Everything Else

Of course, salary negotiation is an obvious opportunity to flex your skills, but there are many other opportunities throughout your career to negotiate. In fact, I would argue that every day, there is at least one thing you are negotiating. Let's talk about some of them.

HOW TO ASK FOR A RAISE

When asking for a raise, you are not asking the company to do you a favour. You're simply asking to be fairly compensated for the value you provide. That's it. It's not personal, just professional, remember?

A common mistake people make is asking for a raise with little data or reasoning. Yes, a well-run company should be adjusting your salary or proactively discussing your compensation with you, but sorry to break it to you: No one is coming to advocate on your behalf. You have to be the hero of your own story. It's up to you to make sure you're paid fairly.

So don't complain, be passive-aggressive, focus on personal needs or gossip, or get defensive. Instead, remember that this is a transactional relationship, and you just want to adjust your compensation to ensure the partnership is equal.

Don't pull your boss aside after a meeting and blurt out: 'I know you're really busy today as we're wrapping up this project, but I haven't had a raise in twelve months and that's not fair.'

Instead, ask your boss if you can put fifteen minutes on their calendar. (You don't have to tell them why . . . if they think you're quitting, is that the worst thing in the world? Sneaky, sneaky, I know.)

When you meet with them, make your objective business case. Pretend you're a caterer for a wedding, and the bride and groom have just decided to upgrade to the top-shelf bar package. You wouldn't just say, 'Okay, but are you planning on paying more or not?' No! You'd say, 'I'd be happy to accommodate your upgrade, and it will cost an additional thirty-five hundred dollars.' The bride and groom are ordering more value, so you are charging them more. It's transactional!

So get into this headspace when you talk to your boss. You are a specialized expert who is providing a service to a company. Your duties and skills have increased, and so your salary needs to reflect this.

Try this: 'Thanks for sitting down with me. I've been here for a little over a year now, and I've really enjoyed all the projects I've been working on. Our ad revenue is up by fifteen per cent and our newsletter has grown by more than five hundred thousand subscribers as a direct result of projects I've led. In the past year, I've also gained more project management skills and more responsibilities regarding who I manage. Considering all this, and the current market average for my role, I'd like to discuss a salary adjustment. I want to ensure that I'm being fairly compensated for my work. Would a ten per cent raise be out of the question?'

Notice that last question. This is called a 'no-facing question.' No-facing questions are powerful because people feel more comfortable saying no than saying yes. If you reverse engineer the question so that when they say no they're actually saying yes, it leaves you in a more powerful position. Another example I love is, 'Would it be unreasonable to discuss an adjustment to my salary?' Again, your boss saying no actually means they are open to a conversation.

If your boss tells you that it's not a good time to adjust your salary, that doesn't mean the conversation is over. Ask for feedback, and then ask when you can revisit the conversation. Put a date on the calendar. Be the squeaky wheel! And I'm sorry to say it, but if they continue to be obstinate, this may be a sign that you need to leave.

Now, let's say that you succeed in getting a raise or you even get an unsolicited raise. Good for you! But what if it's not quite what you were hoping for? You can absolutely negotiate for a higher raise. You might not get it, but it's worth a shot!

Don't: 'I'm sorry, but that's just not gonna cut it.'

Do: 'Thank you. I appreciate the adjustment to my compensation. However, I'm concerned that this doesn't represent my current market value. To be clear, I love this job, and I'm really proud of how I've handled increased responsibilities this past year, like taking over the company newsletter. Based on my research, an increase of seven to eight per cent would be more appropriate for someone with my skill set.'

HOW TO NEGOTIATE NONSALARY COMPENSATION

If you're negotiating your salary and they really won't budge, or you're happy with your salary as is, you can ask the company to sweeten the deal in other ways. There are many forms of compensation besides salary, including start date, job title, annual leave, stock options, employer pension contributions, flexible hours, work-from-home policy and severance. (More on this last one below.) These can be really valuable and worth fighting (okay, negotiating) for.

> **Don't:** 'Well, if you won't give me more money, you've got to give me SOMETHING.'
>
> **Do:** 'Are there any other elements of the compensation package that you can be flexible on?'

Put the ball in their court instead of just asking for something specific. They may have a company-wide policy that they have to adhere to, and then you're left with nothing. If they ask for more details, name the one thing you want the most and have a backup.

> **Don't:** 'Fine, can I at least work from home sometimes so I don't have to pay for so many expensive train tickets?'
>
> **Do:** 'I would love to sign right now. Is it possible to agree on a hybrid work schedule that has me in the office two to three days a week?'

HOW TO NEGOTIATE SEVERANCE DURING AN OFFER

Severance packages are like insurance – or, perhaps more accurately, a prenup. You're hoping you'll never need one, but you'll be so glad you have it if you ever do. Keep in mind that not all companies offer severance. It's not something that's required by law, but rather a perk like a pension plan or stock options. Also know that typical severance packages are one to three weeks of additional pay for every year you've worked at the company, but literally every company has its own formula, so you might as well try to get as much as you can.

> **Don't:** 'I don't mean to be a Debbie Downer, but I'm getting major recession vibes, so I'll need severance in case of a layoff.'
>
> **Do:** 'One thing I wanted to go over was the severance package. Can you break that down for me?'

Now, let's say they offer you one month's pay at 80 per cent, and that's not enough. Try this:

'I'd really like to say yes to this offer right now, but unfortunately in this economy I have to prepare myself and my family for the worst-case scenario. Are you able to adjust that to two months at one hundred per cent pay?'

WOW, GUYS - THAT WAS A LOT! However, I promise that if you start practising these techniques, you will no longer be intimidated by the idea of negotiating and might actually start to get excited about it. Who would have thought?! Now, let's move on to how to communicate professionally when starting the job.

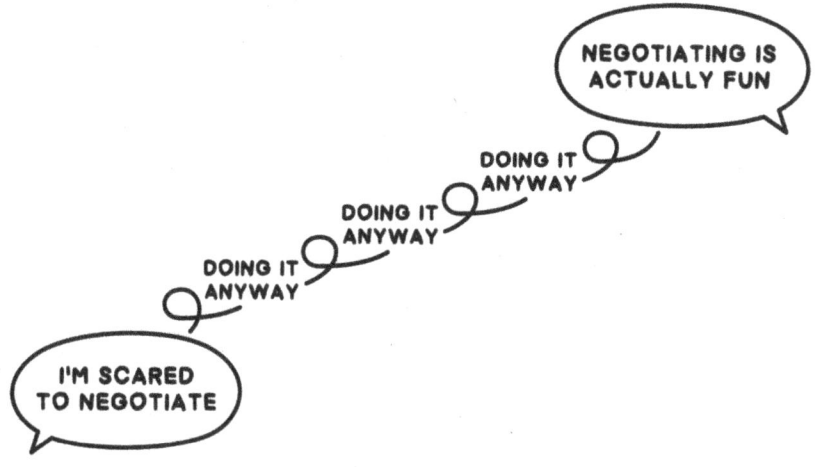

CHAPTER 7

How to Set Boundaries and Expectations

> Tact is the art of making a point without making an enemy.
>
> —HOWARD W. NEWTON

Now that you've successfully negotiated your compensation, it's time to get to work! The first few days on a new job are a crucial time to set expectations and boundaries. Most folks don't know this and jump in feetfirst. I get it, and I know that establishing healthy expectations and boundaries in the beginning might feel uncomfortable. You just want to impress everyone immediately, right away, all the time! But you can absolutely start off on the right foot while making sure you don't set an expectation that will be impossible for you to keep up.

For example, look at Dave. He starts his job at a tech start-up really wanting to win over his boss and colleagues. He shows up to the office at seven every morning and stays until nine each night. If his boss asks him to complete something by the end of the week, he forgoes sleep and does it right away that night.

Dave's boss is thrilled with Dave's performance and quickly starts expecting this level of productivity. There's only one problem – after a few months, Dave is completely burned out. He's exhausted and makes a few careless errors. Then he misses a deadline. Dave's boss calls him in and says, 'You showed so much promise, but I'm really disappointed in you.' This crushes Dave, and he soon comes down with a nasty flu, bringing down his performance even more.

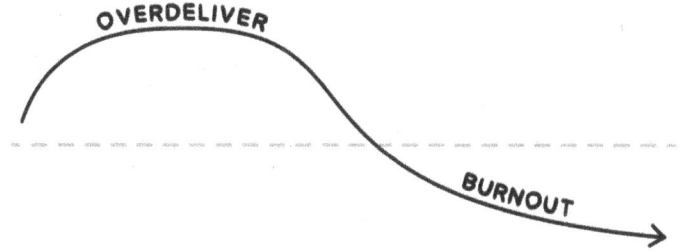

What would have happened if Dave had focused less on proving himself and more on setting healthy, sustainable expectations and boundaries? Of course, you want to make a good impression when you start a job – and you will, by being the rock star that you already are – but it's just as important to start as you mean to go on. Let me show you how.

Your Guide to Your First Ninety Days

Your first ninety days at a new job are key for being proactive about establishing expectations, setting boundaries, and creating a road map to get where you want to go. You are setting the tone and showing people what they can expect from you. The way you speak and carry yourself are the ways that people will expect you to keep speaking and carrying yourself. So it's important to establish right up front whether or not you are someone who stays late, grabs the coffee, and helps everyone out all the time. Show others what they can expect from you, teach them how to treat you, and don't forget to always be polite, professional, clear and kind.

To keep it simple, I like to break this guide to your first ninety days down into thirty-day chunks:

DAYS 1-30

Besides the basic stuff like getting onboarded with HR, completing any necessary training, filling out paperwork and setting up your benefits (yada, yada, yada), this first month is all about getting to know the team and how you are going to work together. One of the best things you can do during this time is to be proactive about meeting your new colleagues. Study the org chart and then reach out to schedule one-on-one coffee chats with everyone you'll be working with directly. This is your chance not only to build relationships and make a good impression, but also to get the tea without directly saying, 'Hey, what's it really like to work with boss guy?'

Try something short, sweet and casual:

Hi Tim!

    My name is Erin McGoff, and I'll be working with you as NPR's new producer on the video team. Would you be available for a 15-minute chat sometime this week or next? I'd love to get your insights on workflow and any advice you have. Wednesday 12–5 p.m. EST is free for me.

    Thanks,

    Erin

Then, during your chat with them, have some thoughtful questions prepared. Try things like:

- 'What is the biggest challenge facing the company/department right now?'
- 'Can you fill me in on what's been going on this year? Anything I should know?'
- 'Our manager seems like a great boss. Do you have any advice for working with her?'
- 'I know we'll be working together on some projects. Is there anything I should know up front regarding workflow and handoff?'
- 'What do you enjoy most about working here?'
- 'Any advice for the new hire? I appreciate any insights you have!'
- 'Who else do you think I should connect with?'
- 'Is there anything I can do to make your job easier?'

During your first thirty days, you should also communicate with your boss about how they like to work. Many people don't even consider doing this, but it can radically change your work life (for the better!). Not all bosses are created equal. Some want constant updates, while others want to be left alone and only informed if there's a problem. Some like to communicate over text, while others prefer email or Slack. It entirely depends on the industry, company, culture and your boss's preferences.

Of course, some bosses might tell you this kind of thing directly, but many don't. So ask! Schedule a one-on-one during your first month on the job and ask questions like:

- 'What is my top priority for the next ninety days?'
- 'If I have a question, do you prefer to be contacted via Slack, email or a quick call?'
- 'How would you describe your management style?'
- 'What should I know about the team's culture and dynamics?'
- 'What is the number one goal for this department in the next twelve months?'
- 'How can I make your job easier?'

Finally, during these first thirty days, start documenting everything. Create a folder on Google Drive (or whatever you like to use) and keep track of everything – feedback, clients, projects, wins, etc. This is a way of gaslight-proofing yourself in case someone questions you later on. It will also be incredibly helpful to pull from this folder when you want to ask for a raise or a promotion (or, you know, apply for a new job).

DAYS 31-60

By now, you should be fully onboarded and in the flow of your day-to-day work life. It's a good idea to expand your in-office network by setting up coffee chats with people from other departments. This will help you learn more about the company, and of course, ABN – always be networking!

If you want to ask someone 'random' to meet with you, try this:

> Hi Tabi!
>
> I'm Erin McGoff, and I recently started as lead producer here at ABC. I'd love to learn more about your work in the finance department and better understand how our departments work together. Would you be open to grabbing a coffee or having a quick virtual chat sometime next week? Wednesday 12–5:00 p.m. EST is open for me!
>
> Best,
> Erin

When you meet with these people, ask them things like:

- 'When did you start working here?'
- 'How has your experience working here been?'
- 'What does your day-to-day look like?'

- 'What are the best and worst parts of your job?'
- 'What is something about [department] in [industry] that everyone should know?'
- 'What is something other departments, maybe like mine, don't get about your department?'
- 'Do you have any advice for me?'

And of course, always remember to thank them for their time!

This is also a great opportunity for you to start setting expectations. If you want people to love working with you, you have to do more than just be great at your job. You also have to be constantly meeting or exceeding expectations. But, and this is a big but, many folks don't know how to properly do this and promptly burn themselves out like Dave. Those folks need to read this book, because I'm about to tell you how to constantly be great to work with, while low-key not doing any more work than you normally would.

Here's the secret: Try to underpromise and overdeliver. Most people do the opposite. They overpromise and underdeliver. Let's look at an example. Brandon is new at his job and eager to impress his boss. So when it comes time to complete his first report, he overpromises. His boss, Rick, asks for the report to be delivered by Friday EOD (end of day), but Brandon says, 'No worries, Rick, I'll have this report to you by Wednesday morning!'

'That's what I like to hear!' his boss replies. Brandon smiles, enjoying the fact that his boss clearly sees his hard work and can-do attitude. Brandon opens his new project, and his jaw drops. *This is way longer than I expected it to be*, he thinks. *The reports at my last job were half this long!*

But Brandon made a promise, and he has to get this report to his boss by Wednesday morning. So he works and works. He stays up late and wakes up early, losing track of what cup of coffee he's on. On Tuesday evening, he realizes it won't be possible to finish this report on top of all the other work he has to do, so he messages his boss.

'Hi Rick, sorry, but this report is way longer than I expected, and I'll have to get it to you by Thursday morning instead of tomorrow. I'm sorry, I should have looked at it before making any promises. I'll do better moving forward. Sorry again.' His boss replies that it's okay, but both Brandon and his boss are feeling a bit deflated. A broken promise isn't the best way to start out a new working relationship.

Now, let's look at what would happen if Brandon underpromised and overdelivered.

This time, when Rick asks for the report to be delivered by Friday morning, Brandon says, 'Friday morning? That's going to be tight, but I'm sure I can make it work.' Rick replies, 'Thanks.' Brandon isn't fazed by not making Rick joyous in this moment, because he knows actions speak louder than words.

Brandon opens the report and sees how long it is. He's glad he didn't overpromise. He gets to work and figures he has the capacity to complete it by Thursday night instead of Friday morning. But he decides to complete it on Thursday night and send it to his boss at 6:00 a.m. on Friday morning, right when his boss requested it. This way, his boss doesn't get used to him submitting things early, but Brandon can still do that on occasion when strategically necessary.

'This looks great,' Rick says on Friday morning. 'Thanks for getting it to me so early. Now I have plenty of time to review before our meeting.' Brandon smiles and says, 'Good luck in your meeting!'

In both scenarios, Brandon did the same amount of work, but in the second scenario, he impressed his boss as opposed to disappointing him. It's all about setting expectations.

Of course, this means that you can't be a people pleaser and say yes to everything. This can be tough in the moment. I know, I hate letting people down too. But it's worth a minute or two of awkwardness in order to get that huge payoff when you deliver early or on time. If you do this, you will build a reputation for getting things done when you say you will, which most bosses and companies value tremendously.

During this time, you also want to establish your boss's expectations for you. This requires good communication. For example, say your boss emails you one evening at 8:00 p.m. asking you to do something 'right away'. What expectation do you want to set? Are you going to respond tonight? Are you going to be available 24/7? Are you always going to be checking your email after 5:00 p.m.?

Here's what you do: Go to your boss the next morning and say, 'Good morning! Would you mind if I ask you about something? I wanted to get on the same page and clarify expectations when it comes to after-hours communication. I saw that your email came through at eight last night, and it was labelled urgent. I wasn't sure if you just send emails as you're working, or if there was an expectation for me to respond to that last night. I wanted to check in with you and get aligned on expectations around availability.'

Hopefully, your boss will say something like, 'Oh, I should have clarified. I don't expect you to be checking your email at home. When I said urgent, I meant today urgent, not last-night urgent. Thanks for checking!'

However, if your boss says, 'I expect you to respond to an urgent email when you get an urgent email,' then we've got some work to do. This is the first test of your boundaries.

Before getting into how to handle this, I'm going to address one thing. If you're in a competitive industry, you need to be competitive. Working in the film industry, I'm on 24/7, and that's because there are other people who want my job. I have to be the best and do what I need to do to get things done.

So, yes, I respond to emails after hours. That's something I'm willing to do because of the type of industry I want to work in. The same is true in other industries like finance, real estate, health care, entrepreneurship, etc. Please use common sense.

However, if you're like most people and work in an industry where not responding to an email after 8:00 p.m. is okay, here's what you can do. First, resist the urge to get angry. You might feel slighted, disrespected and bitter that your boss doesn't respect your personal time. If this is the case, it might be a sign that you need a new boss and/or job. But if this is something you feel you can get past, try something like this:

'Thanks for clarifying. Should we look into adjusting my

work hours to ensure I don't miss any urgent emails? I'm not on the clock at eight p.m., and don't have access to my office phone or email then, so I want to avoid this being a problem moving forward.'

If your boss says, 'That was just one time. We don't need to adjust any hours,' you can reply, 'Good to know. Moving forward, I am unable to check my work email after five thirty p.m., so any urgent emails will be promptly addressed at nine the next morning. Thank you for clarifying with me.' Hopefully, the problem is solved. But if it keeps happening, you have to decide if you're willing to be available at all hours or if you need to start looking for a new job.

DAYS 61-90

Now that you've been on the job for a couple of months, your boss and colleagues are getting a sense of who you are and what your work is like. Likewise, you know the company's systems, policies and workflow. It's a good time to get feedback from your boss on your performance so far.

If your boss hasn't organised a three-month performance appraisal with you, schedule a one-on-one and ask:

'Now that I've hit the ninety-day mark and we've worked together a bit, I'd love to get your feedback on how I'm doing so far. Are there any areas where you think I'm excelling or areas where I could improve? Your input would really help me ensure I'm on the right track and contributing effectively to the team!'

This is also a good time to be open with your boss about your goals. Before your meeting, come up with two or three goals for the next six to twelve months. What do you want to accomplish? Share this info with your boss and ask for their support to help you reach these goals.

For example, try saying:

'Thanks for the feedback. I also wanted to share a few goals and get your thoughts on them. Is that all right? In the next six to twelve months I'm focused on mastering our project management tools, building strong relationships with our clients, and ensuring smooth execution of our current builds. Then over the next few years, I'd like to work my way up to take on more responsibility, and eventually to bring in new business by working with the marketing department in a leadership role. I'd love to hear your feedback!'

How to Set and Reinforce Professional Boundaries

Boundaries are invisible lines that define what behaviours are acceptable to you. When someone's behaviour is okay with you, it falls within those lines. When it's not okay, it falls outside those lines. In general, setting and reinforcing boundaries are essential for maintaining healthy relationships. It's basically the only way for people to know how you like to be treated and what is acceptable to you. Setting boundaries at work is an important way of advocating for yourself.

Of course, where you put those lines and the exact boundaries you set is up to you. Some people want to be close to their bosses and colleagues and bring their whole selves to work.

This is your right, but I urge you to be cautious here. If you want to bring your whole self to work, don't be surprised when work expects your whole self and therefore doesn't respect your boundaries. In my opinion, it's much cleaner and wiser to keep your personal and professional lives separate.

Unfortunately, setting a boundary isn't a one-and-done thing. It's usually a process of setting and then consistently reinforcing a boundary. Each time you reinforce a boundary, you are standing up for yourself and protecting your peace. Here's how to do it.

HOW TO SET BOUNDARIES WITH YOUR BOSS

Farrah works at a media company, where the boundaries in general are pretty loose. When she is hired by her boss, Carla, Farrah is over the moon to be working for someone so cool and fun and interesting. Carla is an icon in the industry, and Farrah looks up to her as a mentor and role model. Being single, Farrah often gossips with Carla on Mondays about her weekends and her dating life. This is fun and doesn't bother Farrah at all, until it starts interfering with her career.

After about a year on the job, Farrah gets into a relationship with John. Of course, Carla knows all about their dates and future plans. Then one weekend, Carla asks Farrah to create a deck for a new brand the company is launching. 'I'm so sorry,' Farrah says, 'but I can't this weekend.' Carla responds, 'I know you and John were planning to go away this weekend, but can't you just push it to next weekend? I really need your help with this.'

Suddenly, it doesn't feel good for Carla to know so much about Farrah's personal life. Instead, it feels like it's being used against her. But Farrah brushes it aside and moves on. About six months later, Farrah has her annual review and tells Carla that her goal is to be promoted within the next year. 'Okay, we'll see,' Carla says with a smile. 'But with the way things are going, I suspect you might be busy with wedding planning over the next year!' Farrah is (rightfully) furious and realizes that it was a mistake not to set a boundary with Carla in the beginning.

Likewise, if you think it's a good idea to be besties with your boss, I want you to think again. Sure, you want them to like you, and it's great if you like them too, but I strongly encourage you not to get too close. There are a few reasons for this.

One, when your boss gets uber comfortable with you being in your current position, she is motivated to keep you there instead of promoting you. This can lead you to stagnate in your role. There's nothing worse than a boss who doesn't want to promote you because she loves your funny stories and just enjoys having you around. That's not the kind of indispensable that you want to be!

Also, if your boss knows too much about your personal life,

they can use it against you, just like Carla did. You don't want your boss saying, 'Oh, you don't need another vacation – didn't you just go to the Bahamas last month?' That's really none of her business, and it's exactly what I mean when I say to be careful about bringing your whole self to work.

Here's an example. Say that on Friday, your boss asks you to come in or complete a work task over the weekend. You have plans to go to a concert out of town. *Don't* tell your boss every detail. In fact, keep it vague! Try: 'Sorry, I'm not available this weekend. In the future, I can make sure I'm available if I have prior notice.'

Now, a good boss will say, 'Okay, I understand. Thanks, anyway!' But, let's be real – you may or may not have a good boss. She could say something like, 'Well, why not? I really need you to be a team player instead of just leaving me hanging.'

If this happens, do not take the bait and say, 'Lady, get over yourself. I don't want to work this weekend!!' Instead, try this: 'Oh no, I hope you don't see it that way. I would say I am a team player, as I've happily jumped in to help in the past. I'm just unavailable to work this particular weekend.' Then reiterate, 'In the future, I'd be happy to help out if I have notice in advance.'

It's really important to enforce this boundary, or your boss might get used to you being available at the last minute, and I'm guessing that you don't want to set that expectation.

THE BIG STICK THEORY OF BOUNDARIES

In 1901, President Theodore Roosevelt famously said, 'Speak softly and carry a big stick.' Of course, Teddy was talking about his approach to foreign policy, but I think this statement applies just as well to setting boundaries at work. The 'speak softly' bit is being kind to people by default, and the 'big stick' part is being unmistakably direct. This means drawing firm boundaries, setting clear expectations, and having zero tolerance for BS.

Kind communication with strong boundaries is a super weapon in your strategic communication tool kit. Making other people feel understood, heard and supported is powerful, and it's not something that just anyone can do. However, don't ever let people mistake your kindness for weakness. Be kind, but let people know when they have crossed a boundary. If you feel that someone is disrespecting or taking advantage of your kindness, it's time to pull out the big stick.

Take me, for example. I am a friendly, petite, blonde, kind person. Some might even assume I'm a pushover. But make no mistake: The moment I suspect that someone is trying to take advantage of my kindness, I pull out the big stick and make sure they know who they are dealing with.

Let's say I'm in a meeting with a coworker I'm supposed to be collaborating with on a new pitch. Imagine they are being a little flirty, a little suggestive, saying cringy things like, 'I'm sure someone who looks like you will have no problem selling this pitch.' This is a new coworker, so I'm not sure if this is just their personality or if it's specifically directed at me, but I'm going to give them the benefit of the doubt and continue our meeting. I may hint at my discomfort and redirect, saying something neutral like, 'Oh, okay . . . so, anyway, let's look at the key outcomes slide again . . .'

Then towards the end of the meeting, they say something completely unprofessional and suggestive. This time, there's no question about it: They have crossed my line in the sand. They are clearly taking advantage of my kindness and trying to assert some type of dominance by making me uncomfortable. This is something I don't tolerate, and now it's time to bring out the big stick.

'I'm not sure what I did to give you the impression that you can speak to me this way, but you can't. I'm here to get this pitch completed and win new business, and that's it. I'd appreciate it if you gave me the same professional courtesy I am giving you.' Silence. And a report in writing to HR.

HOW TO SET BOUNDARIES WITH COWORKERS

My hot take, which you may disagree with, is that you shouldn't be friends with your coworkers. Sure, you may develop true, lasting friendships with a small handful of coworkers throughout your life, but in general, keeping your professional and personal lives separate will protect you from so many professional and personal problems.

This doesn't mean that you have to be cold or rude or avoid ever speaking to your coworkers. You can absolutely be friendly without getting super close. Go on the coffee dates, chat it up in the office and develop camaraderie. But I would recommend stopping short of telling them your darkest secrets, spending time together over the weekend, or letting your coworkers become your entire social circle.

One boundary that's really important to set is around workplace gossip and drama. Do not let yourself be sucked into these! I don't care if you have the hottest tea on the planet. Keep it to yourself. Spill it to your nonwork friends (or to me) if you're literally going to burst. But pretty much any time you gossip at work, it will come back to bite you. I promise.

The key to staying out of workplace gossip and drama is unfortunately to be really boring. I'm not saying you have to be boring at work all the time. In fact, try to avoid that. But when someone tries to rope you into drama, get real boring for a minute and do not engage.

For example, say a coworker asks you, 'Did you hear about Jack and Diane? Reshma saw them leaving together the other night, and I think there's something going on.' Don't say, 'Oh, wow, I saw them huddled together in the break room the other day! This is so exciting!'

Even if you're dying inside about how cute Jack and Diane would be together, act really disinterested. Say something completely neutral like, 'Oh, cool,' in a bored tone, and then say, 'Well, I've got to get back to work!' If you keep this up, your coworker is going to get sick of trying to gossip with you and will find someone who is willing to engage. Let her!

Now, let's say that a coworker takes it a step further and really tries to pull you directly into a drama. For example, she asks, 'Why are you working with Jessica on that project? You know I don't like her, and she's a total backstabber.' Again, do not engage. Do not ask for details about Jessica's backstabbing. Do not defend her, do not get emotional, and do not defend yourself. Keep it neutral and straightforward: 'Oh, it's just part of my job.'

Of course, you will have to tailor your exact response to fit the specific situation, but in any case of workplace drama or gossip, the key is simply not to engage. Don't take the bait. Don't even nibble on it. Keep it neutral and direct and respectful, and then get back to the whole reason you're there in the first place – you know, your job!

HOW TO SET BOUNDARIES WITH A CLIENT

If you're a freelancer, solopreneur, or someone with a side hustle, it's extremely important to set boundaries with your clients. The real key here is having everything locked down in writing. That's how you set the boundary in the first place. In-

HOW TO SET BOUNDARIES AND EXPECTATIONS

vest in hiring a lawyer to create a boilerplate contract that you can then tailor to specific projects. I promise this will be worth it.

Then, of course, you have to reinforce that boundary. For example, say a client is asking for extra work or rounds of revisions that are beyond what's stated in the contract. Don't just assume that this client is trying to take advantage or squeeze free work out of you. Most of the time, they just don't remember or don't have a clear understanding of what the contract says. It's always in your best interest to give people the benefit of the doubt and be straightforward. Of course, this is why it's so important to have everything in writing in the first place! The terms of your contract are objective, not personal or emotional.

Simply say, 'I'd be happy to do that! However, this is outside the scope of our contract, so going forward my rate for this would be X.' The key here is to offer solutions. Perhaps, 'If you will continue needing updates going forward, I'd be happy to provide a package for you,' or 'If you have flexibility on turnaround time, I can give you a ten per cent discount.' By reinforcing a boundary, you'll be solving a problem for your client and getting yourself more money and more work!

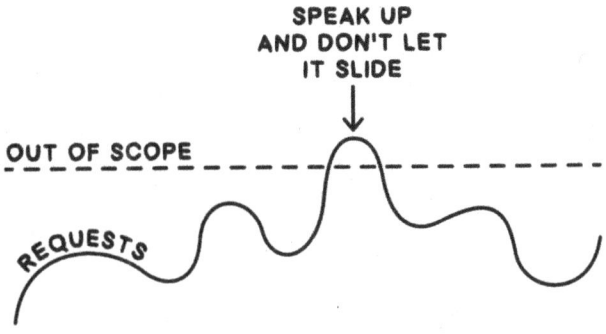

SETTING THE RIGHT boundaries and expectations at work will protect your peace and make every day on the job easier. But an ambitious go-getter like you needs to take another step in order to steer your career in the direction you want. Next up, we'll talk about how to do this by advocating for yourself – kindly and professionally, of course.

CHAPTER 8

How to Advocate for Yourself Without Being a Jerk

Don't raise your voice, improve your argument.
—DESMOND TUTU

The word 'advocate' actually means to support or argue for a particular cause. For example, a politician can advocate for a certain policy change. When it comes to your career, you are your own cause! Steering your career in the direction you want it to go is your top priority. No one is going to do this for you. In order to get things moving in your direction, you are the first domino that needs to fall. So a huge part of your job at work is to support or argue for yourself. In other words, advocate!

Let's take a look at Sarah and Emily, who are both hired as junior publicists at a boutique PR firm and start within a few weeks of each other. Both women are driven and qualified, but they have very different approaches to their jobs. Sarah is very proactive. She schedules coffee chats with her new colleagues, asks questions to find out how her boss likes to work

and communicate, and makes her goals very clear. She tells her boss that she wants to gain more responsibilities and become a full-time publicist within a year.

Emily, on the other hand, has similar ambitions, but is concerned that being so direct will come off as overly eager, aggressive and prideful. She figures that if she works hard and goes above and beyond, her boss will notice and admire her humility and determination. So she keeps her head down and focuses on her work. And she does do a good job, but she's just one member of a larger team, so her work isn't that visible to leadership.

When the company signs a new client, their boss picks Sarah to take the lead, knowing that she is eager to take on more responsibilities. Emily is disappointed, but what can she do? She figures that if she keeps putting in the work, she'll get picked for the next one. She just needs to be patient.

Sarah's new client is very high profile, so their boss pays close attention to Sarah's work, which is successful. At the end of that first year, Sarah is promoted to full-time publicist and receives a nice bump in salary, while Emily, despite being the first one in the office and the last to leave, remains in her role as junior publicist.

Just imagine what might happen over the next few years if Sarah and Emily stay on their current trajectories. Sarah's ability to speak up and advocate for herself set her on a completely different path. Unless Emily learns to advocate for herself, she is likely to remain stagnant and frustrated in her career.

Well, I'm not going to let this happen to you! Like Sarah, you are your own best advocate. Unfortunately, you can't expect someone else to go out on a limb for you if you don't ask them to. You have to be willing to go out on a limb for yourself. People like to help people on a mission, people who are proactive, assertive, and know what they want – and aren't afraid to ask for it.

You are about to become one of these people. In this chapter, I am going to teach you how to advocate for yourself on the job in a way that will set you on a path towards your goals, whether you are just starting a new job or have been in your role for some time. You'll learn how to clarify your goals, gain visibility and stand up for yourself to get what you want.

Best of all, you are going to learn how to do all these things in a way that is professional, admirable and true to who you are. Remember, you do not need to be a passive pushover in order to be kind and polite, and you do not have to be rude or obnoxious to be a top dog. So let's go get it.

> **KIND AND EFFECTIVE WAYS OF SAYING NO AT WORK**
>
> Sure, 'No' is a complete sentence, but sometimes you want to add a few more words onto that sentence in order to be as professional, polite and assertive as possible. Try these:
>
> - 'I don't have the capacity to prioritize that at the moment.'
> - 'I can't right now, but I'll take a look when I can.'
> - 'I'm currently occupied with X. Can this wait?'
> - 'I'm currently working on X. What would you like me to prioritize?'
> - 'My plate is full at the moment, but I'm happy to help if something clears up.'
> - 'Sorry, I'm unavailable.'

> - 'Sorry, my schedule is full right now.'
> - 'That unfortunately isn't possible. Can we do X instead?'
> - '[Coworker] might be a better resource for that.'

How to Advocate for Yourself During Every One-on-One with Your Boss

Most people don't realize that every one-on-one meeting with the boss is a great opportunity to be proactive about your career and to advocate for yourself and your goals. So most of the time, they end up going something like this:

Boss: 'Hi Erin, how have things been?'

Erin: 'Everything has been fine, no issues on my end.' Then maybe you'll waste some time going through your to-do list for the rest of the week. What did you accomplish? Nothing!

Instead, be proactive! This is a four-step process:

1. Before your one-on-one, send your boss an email with updates, a few (three to four) topics you want to touch base on and any wins or challenges you've experienced since you last met.

2. Then, start the meeting by asking your boss what's on their mind. This will help clear their cognitive load and take care of anything urgent. You can try, 'Is there anything specific on your mind that you'd like to discuss?'

3. Next, you want to update your boss on your accomplishments and any challenges you've experienced. Remember to keep it professional and positive (and brief)! You're not there to complain about how difficult things were. This is about showing your boss how beautifully you've handled obstacles. If you have run into any challenges you haven't been able to get past, bring this up to your boss, but be sure to keep it professional. Instead of, 'This software keeps breaking and it's driving me insane and wasting my time,' try something like, 'I'd like to discuss our cloud systems – they glitch three to four times a day, backing up our workload and putting our data at risk. I've tried to troubleshoot, but as you know, this is a continual problem. Could we explore new cloud solutions this week? I can take that on.'

4. Finally, you want to make sure that you and your boss are aligned on your goals moving forward. Of course, your exact script will depend on your goals, but try something like this: 'I know our next check-in is on December 12, and we're really focused on getting our newsletter up and running, so my action items are researching platforms, designing a schedule, and outlining topics. Does that cover everything?' Hopefully, your boss responds with,

'Yep! Wow, you are such a good employee I'm gonna give you a gazillion-dollar raise and a five-year vacation.'

How to Ask for a Promotion

Positioning yourself for a promotion actually starts way before a promotion opportunity in your company comes around. In fact, I recommend that you start advocating for yourself a full year before you ask for that promotion. Yes, a year! And at the beginning of that year, you want to make your goals very clear to your boss so they can help you get there. Here's what you do:

Schedule a one-on-one with your boss and come prepared with lots of data. Remember that folder I asked you to start to keep track of all your accomplishments and projects? This is when you need it! Say to your boss, 'I've really enjoyed the work I've been doing over the past six months. In that time, I've successfully taken the lead on three accounts, and our team has increased our revenue by twenty per cent. By this time next year, I want to be at the director level, and I'm willing to do what it takes. Can you help me create a road map to get there?'

A good boss will appreciate this and work with you to help you reach your goals. So don't come at me saying, 'But, Erin, I tried this, and it didn't work!' Unfortunately, not all bosses are good, and not all companies want you to advance. Even the best career advice in the world isn't going to work at a toxic organization! If you're using these techniques and doing great work and aren't advancing, I'm sorry to say that it might be time for you to leave.

In the meantime, you can also use this script if an opportunity comes up and you do not receive a promotion. If this happens, schedule a one-on-one with your boss. During the meeting, keep it factual and not emotional. Don't talk about who got promoted instead of you and how unfair that is.

Instead, say, 'I've really enjoyed the work I've been doing over the past six months. In that time, I've successfully taken the lead on three accounts, and our team has increased our revenue by twenty per cent. I was not promoted this time, but by this time next year, I want to be at the director level, and I'm willing to do what it takes. Can you help me create a road map to get there?'

Another time you may want to ask for a promotion is when your boss is leaving. Of course, you want their job, and you'd be perfect for it. But then something gross happens, like HR asks if you can train the person they're hiring. It's enough to make you want to start flipping tables, right? Don't do that.

Instead, calmly say, 'I was actually hoping to be considered to fill that position. If you're open to it, I'd really like to be considered. I can jump right in, no training or onboarding necessary. If you have any hesitations about my ability to perform in the role, I'd be happy to discuss with the team.'

Then there may be times when you want to ask for a title change to more accurately reflect the work you're already doing. Your ability to get a title change will vary depending on the type of company you work for. For example, if it's a big, well-established company, they most likely have clear roles, titles and policies. You would have to come up with a very clear case to get a title change, cross-referencing your current duties with those of another role. But it's still worth having the conversation. If you work for a small company or a start-up, it's much more likely that they can be flexible with the title.

For example, say that you start a new job as a graphic designer, and then your boss asks you to do all the branding for the company. This is not what you signed up for, but you figure it's a small start-up, and you can take a stab at it. It turns out that you enjoyed it and feel confident doing this work. Great! Now it's time to advocate for yourself by asking for a title change. Here's how:

Go to your boss and say, 'I enjoyed doing this work, and am really happy to have been trusted with this responsibility, but it's actually out of scope for the title of graphic designer. Typically, a graphic designer would focus more on day-to-day tasks, but when it comes to the branding for the company, that's a much more senior role. However, I am completely up to the challenge if you're open to discussing an adjustment to my title. For these responsibilities, the title of brand manager, brand designer or lead designer would all be appropriate.'

WHAT TO DO WHEN SOMEONE KEEPS INTERRUPTING YOU

There's nothing more annoying than a coworker constantly interrupting you, but this is another situation where we have to give a little grace. Interruptions happen. We've all done it. I've done it. You've done it.

Seriously, I know you have, and you probably didn't mean anything by it. So if it happens once or twice, I recommend letting it go. But of course, don't just let yourself be talked over on a consistent basis.

If there's that one annoying coworker who keeps doing this, you have a few options:

1. Just keep talking through their interruption. Keep going, and pretend like you don't hear them. It'll be awkward, and that's okay. Let it be awkward, and they'll eventually stop and look like the bad guy.

2. Say one of the following:
    - 'Please let me finish, I was saying ...'
    - 'Can I finish my point really quick? As I was saying ...'
    - 'One sec – almost done with my point! So ...'

3. If this is a consistent problem, you can take a more assertive approach. First, privately pull aside your coworker and ask them if it's a good time to talk. Then, if it is, let them know how you feel.

    Try this: 'Thanks for giving me a few minutes to chat. I've noticed that in recent meetings you've been interrupting people, especially me, very frequently. I'd really appreciate it if you could be more cognisant of this, as it's making it difficult for me to get my points across and be heard. Have you noticed this as well?'

> 4. Ending with a question makes the feedback less accusatory and makes it more likely that the other person will be receptive. If it persists, keep addressing it in the moment: 'Please do not interrupt me; I'm still speaking. As I was saying...'

How to Make Yourself More Visible

Of course, the best way to set yourself up for that promotion you want is to make sure you're doing visible, high-profile work and getting credit for it. This all comes down to being assertive.

For example, let's say that your boss congratulates your co-worker Jane on the great newsletter when you're actually the one who wrote it. Don't scream, 'What are you talking about?! I wrote that entire newsletter! Jane just sat in the corner Snapchatting some guy and eating Chipotle.'

Instead, go to your boss and try this:

'Hey, boss, do you have a minute? I'm really happy that you were satisfied with the newsletter. I just checked the analytics, and we had a sixty per cent open rate and a four per cent click-through rate, which is great. You may not realize that while Jane did help with the outlining, I actually did end up writing and designing the entire newsletter myself.'

Don't throw Jane under the bus! If your boss says, 'Oh, really?

Huh. I saw her name on the project,' you can say, 'Yes, but in order to get it done right and on time, I jumped in. I really enjoyed doing it, and am very happy that it's a success. I'd be happy to officially lead these moving forward.' Trust me, your boss will get the hint.

Likewise, if a coworker volunteers to lead a project that you want, don't exclaim, 'But you get all the good projects! That's not fair!!' Don't just let her have it either, though. Simply say, 'I would also like to be considered.'

Now, if you happen to work in a very competitive workplace, it might be better to go directly to your boss. Reference that handy folder again, and lead with facts. 'I've successfully run three comparable campaigns in the past year, and I think I'd be a strong project manager for this client.'

Sometimes, unfair things will happen, and you have to make sure that you continue to advocate for yourself during these times too. For example, what should you do if your boss decides to put someone else on an account that you've been working on for over a year? When something so unfair, stupid and wrong is happening, it's easy to turn into a boiling bucket of rage juice. But it always benefits you to stay calm and strategic.

Go to your boss and say, 'Oh, you're moving the Peterson account to Jim?' But say it like they're putting orange juice on their cereal – like, 'Bro, are you okay?' Your boss will probably say something like, 'Yeah, we have to do some reshuffling,' but don't just let it go.

Your goal here is to align your boss's desires (making the client happy) with your desire (not wanting to lose the account). You can say, 'Of course, and as much as I value being a team player, I am concerned about the effect this will have on the client. I know they're looking to extend their contract, and I've developed a great relationship with them. I'd like to stay on. I can do a great job managing them, and I'm open for feedback on anything I can improve on.'

NOW THAT YOU are a pro at advocating for yourself, it's all smooth sailing from here, right? Yeah, unfortunately, no. In any job, there will always be bumps in the road and uncomfortable, unfair and/or downright yucky situations that you find yourself in. But next up, I am going to give you the words to gracefully handle the trickiest workplace scenarios with ease.

CHAPTER 9

How to Deal with Sticky Situations

Effective communication is 20 per cent what you know and 80 per cent how you feel about what you know.

—JIM ROHN

No matter how well you do your job or how professionally you communicate, you are going to run into some awkward situations, drama, and maybe even full-blown conflicts at work. That's the bad news. The good news, however, is that when you learn the right words to handle these situations in a kind and professional way, they will be nothing more than little blips on your radar.

For example, Dina works at a design firm and bills clients hourly for her work designing their websites. One day, she hands her boss her list of billable hours for the week. He hands it back to her and says, 'Please add seven hours on the Blumberg account for copywriting services.'

Dina pauses, unsure of what to say. She manages this account and has zero knowledge of any copywriting services being fulfilled. Is her boss asking her to overcharge the client?

At this moment, Dina has a few choices. She can just say, 'Okay...' and do something she feels uncomfortable with. Or she can jump to conclusions and scream, 'How dare you ask me to do something unethical like that?'

Instead, she pauses and makes sure she has all the information. 'Oh,' she says, 'I didn't realize they had asked for help with copywriting. Did we provide those services?'

'Don't worry about it,' her boss says with a smile. 'This is just how it's done. Thanks, Dina,' and he dismisses her.

Now Dina is really torn. Her boss is asking her to do something that she considers morally wrong and that she doesn't want to do, but she also doesn't want to come off as judgemental or be pegged as problematic. So Dina makes sure to stay focused on her desired outcome in this situation – not to have to overbill the client.

'I understand that's how it's done,' Dina says, making a point of using 'I' statements and not accusing her boss of anything, 'but I'm not comfortable with it. Is there someone in copywriting you can ask instead?'

Sure, there are some bosses who might fly off the handle at this and accuse Dina of being self-righteous. If this was the case, Dina would probably have to start looking for a new job. She doesn't want to work at a company that's not aligned with her values, anyway. Luckily, her boss is more reasonable and doesn't push the issue. 'Sure,' he says simply, and Dina doesn't hear anything about this again.

Of course, there are an infinite number of potential sticky

situations like this that you might face at work. It would be impossible to cover all of them in this book. In this chapter, I'll cover as many as I can, but I also want to share a basic framework that can help in any and every sticky scenario:

Step 1 is to think about your desired outcome and be specific. In other words, what is the exact action that you want taken? Do you want your boss to go to HR and tell them to give you a raise? Do you want your coworker to stop using your mug? You get the idea. This is not about making a point or teaching someone a lesson, as tempting as that may be! It's about resolving a specific issue productively and professionally.

Step 2 is to think about the emotions you're experiencing and the stories you may be telling yourself about this situation. For example, if your boss has been saying for over a year that she's going to give you a raise and it hasn't come through yet, you're probably feeling a lot of anger and resentment. And you might be making assumptions like 'My boss hates me.' This is just a story you're telling yourself. For all you know, your boss has been fighting for you hard with the finance department, but they're stonewalling her. Try to stay objective and keep yourself from making any assumptions.

Step 3 is to approach the situation with radical empathy and give the other person the benefit of the doubt. Imagine that the tables were turned, and ask yourself how you would want the other person to handle things if they were in your shoes. Approaching people and situations by trying to see things from their perspective will almost always help you get to your desired outcome.

Between this framework and the scripts below, you'll soon

be handling potentially crazy-making, stress-inducing, keep-you-up-at-night situations with grace and ease. I've broken these down into three main categories: sticky job-offer situations, sticky situations with your coworkers, and sticky situations with your boss. Then we'll tackle microaggressions and other inappropriate behaviour, and how to give and receive feedback without it becoming a sticky situation for either party. Let's go.

Sticky Job-Offer Situations

HOW TO HANDLE A JOB OFFER WHEN YOU'RE WAITING TO HEAR BACK FROM ANOTHER COMPANY

Let's say you've applied and interviewed for jobs as a marketing manager at both Netflix and Hulu. You really liked the team and the vibe better at Netflix, but Hulu reaches out after the interview to offer you the job. Yay! But also, wait – what about Netflix? Can you tell Hulu, 'Actually, I'm waiting to hear back on another job that I want a teensy bit more, so can you just hang tight for a while?' No. No, you cannot.

Here's what you can (and should) say, instead:

Dear Hulu,

Thank you so much for the offer! I'm so excited that you want me to join the team. Can you please send me the offer letter in writing so I can look it over?

Thanks so much,

Erin

This will buy you some time. Then reach out to Netflix with an email like this:

Dear Kelly,

I applied for the marketing manager position and interviewed with you on November 11. I wanted to let you know that I have received another job offer. Transparently, Netflix is my first choice, and I would still love the opportunity to work with you. Are you able to update me on your hiring decision?

Thank you so much,

Erin

Simultaneously, start negotiating with Hulu. Yes, this is completely ethical. Don't worry that you're 'leading them on', even if your heart is with Netflix. You're still negotiating in good faith because the job at Netflix might not come through, and you very well might end up at Hulu. Go back to chapter 6 for a refresher on how to handle this negotiation!

If Netflix does come through with an offer, that's amazing! You could just take it. But remember what I taught you about having two offers – you now have the ultimate leverage! You can negotiate with both companies simultaneously and then go with the one that ends up offering the best package. Of course, you can also choose to go with Netflix even if their final offer is lower. It's not all about money, folks. If both offers are good, it's okay to go with the lower-paying one if it means you'll be happier.

If, however, Netflix tells you that they've decided to hire

someone else, make sure to thank them and wish them the best. Then decide what's best for you. Most likely, you'll wrap up your negotiations with and accept the job at Hulu. Congrats!

HOW TO NEGOTIATE A START DATE

Let's say you got that new job offer. Way to go! They want to know what date you can start. Ideally, you'd love to take a couple of weeks off between jobs. But how do you tell them, 'I could technically start on the sixth, but I'm kinda tired and would actually love to just chill until the eighteenth, so...'

If this happens, you can just say, 'I'm available to start on the eighteenth.' Don't tell them that you're actually leaving your job on the fourth and need some downtime. Just say it as if your job is making you stay until the seventeenth, and the eighteenth is the soonest you can possibly start.

Remember, your employer isn't entitled to the details. And you're not lying – you're telling them when you can start. It's possible that they'll ask, 'Are you able to start any sooner?' Then how you respond is up to you. You can say, 'Sure, does the eleventh work?' and just take one week off between jobs. Or you can say, 'No, unfortunately the twenty-fourth is the earliest I can get started.' If you like, you could throw in something like, 'But I'm happy to get started with onboarding materials on the eighteenth.' Again, up to you!

HOW TO HANDLE STARTING A NEW JOB WHEN YOU HAVE A VACATION ALREADY PLANNED

Sometimes, the job hunting and interviewing process takes longer than you expected, and you can't put your life on hold the entire time. You still have to live and plan and do things. So what happens when you finally get an offer and have a trip planned for right around the time they want you to start? A lot of companies have policies against employees taking time off during their first few months on the job. Does this mean you have to cancel your vacation? Not necessarily.

The key here is to wait until the offer letter is signed and the onboarding process is starting. Of course, please use common sense. If this is a contract temp job where you are needed urgently, obviously let them know sooner! However, if it's a permanent role where there is some flexibility in the start date, sign the offer letter, then bring up your unavailability during onboarding. Remember not to get weighed down by the details. As far as they need to know, you aren't going to Cancun – you have a 'prior commitment'. You aren't going on a cruise – you have a 'preplanned event'.

Try something like this:

Dear Hiring Manager,

I'm so excited about joining the team! I'm wondering if we can discuss my onboarding timeline. I see here that my start date is listed as June 2, which works with my schedule. However, I have a prior commitment that means I'll be out of town from June 9–13. So we can either keep my start date as the second and I'll be out for those days, or we can push my start date to Monday, June 16. Both options work for me, so please let me know which you prefer.

Thanks so much,

Erin

HOW TO HANDLE THE OLD BAIT AND SWITCH

Sadly, sometimes when you start a new job, it doesn't turn out to be exactly what you were expecting . . . or what you were promised. The work you're being given is either a better fit for someone more senior or more junior . . . or someone entirely different. Either way, it's not what you signed up for.

For example, let's say you start a job as a video editor, and then early on your boss tells you that they're between producers and they need you to step up and take on some administrative tasks, like invoicing clients and managing inventory. I recommend that with your positive, collaborative spirit, you try to make this work at first and see how temporary it really is. But say over the next few weeks, you realize you're not doing much video editing at all, but rather fulfilling the duties of an office manager. Do you march into your boss's office and say, 'Uh, this is not what I signed up for!!!'? Yes! But in a more professional way.

Try going to your boss and saying:

'Hey, boss, I've been here for about thirty days, and I'm loving the team and the clients, but I accepted this job under the pretext that I'd be doing editing work, as that's my specialty. According to the job description and what we discussed in the interviews, eighty per cent of my job is meant to be directly related to editing. But so far, I've spent about ninety per cent of my time invoicing and managing inventory. I'm afraid my skills aren't being utilized.'

Hopefully, your boss will hear you and make adjustments so that you are able to start doing the job you signed up for. If not, ask if your boss would mind you scheduling a meeting with HR to help resolve the problem. If the problem is not resolved, it is crucial that you find a new position as soon as possible. This is not the right role for you. It's disappointing, but don't waste your time here. Move on.

Sticky Situations with Coworkers

Unfortunately, no matter how strong your boundaries are or how on point your communication may be, working with humans is going to be at least a little bit fraught some of the time. You spend a lot of time together, your ability to do your job well often depends on them doing their job well, and personalities are bound to clash. But with your collaborative attitude and these scripts, you are going to be able to handle these blips without breaking a sweat.

HOW TO DEAL WITH A LAZY AND UNPROFESSIONAL COWORKER

Lazy, inefficient and/or unproductive people can really drive you crazy. Sometimes you'll work with someone who just makes you think, 'How the heck did you even get past the first interview?' Unfortunately, you are not in control of other people. The only thing you can control is you. It's so important to keep that in mind in all aspects of your life!

If you find yourself in proximity to a downright lazy coworker, the first thing you need to do is ask yourself if this person's laziness is truly affecting you and your ability to do your job. If not, you have to ignore it. I know, I know – it's hard. It's annoying to watch someone else act in a way that is so different from how you choose to carry yourself – but again, it's not your job to fix them. Their choices will result in their consequences. Vent to your friends at happy hour, tell your therapist, or buy a stress ball if you need to.

But remember: You never know the full story. Often, you just can't tell what someone else is going through. As always, give them the benefit of the doubt. We all go through rough periods in our lives, and we remember the people who gave us space and grace when we do. You aren't their parent, and you're not even their friend. You are their coworker. And if they aren't affecting your duties, it's best to ignore them (or check in on them if you're concerned).

But what if a coworker's laziness is indeed negatively affecting your ability to do your job? For example, they need to get you something so you can take the next step in a project, and they often get their piece to you late. In this case, it *is* something you have to address. You might be tempted to go to your boss and tattle, 'Josh isn't doing like any of his work and it's making me deliver projects late, and it's literally not even my fault, he's just lazy and incompetent.'

Before you try that, let's look at a more effective way to

handle this. As usual, I recommend going directly to the source first. Remember: desired outcome. You aren't trying to teach this person a lesson on integrity or character. You want them to change their current behaviour so it doesn't affect your work. That's it.

Ask your coworker if they have a few minutes to talk about workflow. Don't get mad; get curious. Try this:

'I've noticed that when you send me invoices, they're late more than half the time. Then I can't bill the client on time, and it leads to a domino effect. This has been really hard for me to manage. Is there something going on that's causing this to happen? Is there anything I can do?'

This person will likely respond one of two ways. They might say something defensive, along the lines of 'You're not my boss,' or 'I'm doing the best I can,' or 'I'm too busy with other things. Can't you just do this yourself?' This would obviously be the worst-case scenario, and it requires you to keep pressing. Remember to avoid accusatory language like 'You're making me look bad!' Instead, say, 'When you [blank], I feel [blank].' Ideally, it would go like this:

'Is there anything we can do to tighten up this workflow?'

'I'm doing the best I can! I'm busy, and invoicing isn't really part of my job.' You know they're probably justified in their anger, since the company did just conduct layoffs, but it's also not your problem. Everyone has to do their job, and this coworker's job is delivering invoices on time.

'I hear you. Things have been stressful for me too. The only thing is, when the invoices come to me late, I get in trouble for billing the clients late, so it leads to this domino effect. Do you think we could discuss this with our boss since this is something we're both struggling with?'

Again, in any conflict, it's best to try to make your opponent your ally. The more tension you defuse, the more clearly you can see the problem. With problematic people, you can't strong-arm your way to reason. You have to soften them to get them to participate.

Another likely response from this person is, 'Yeah, sorry, I've been [insert excuse] and that's why I've been slacking. I'll get the invoices to you on time going forward.' Hopefully, they mean it, and the problem is resolved. What might happen, however, is that they make a false promise and continue to deliver late. In this scenario, you have to bring this matter up to your boss and simply explain how it's affecting workflow.

During your next one-on-one with your manager or boss, try something like, 'Hey, one more thing, I've been struggling a little bit when it comes to handoff with Bill. He's been delivering invoices a few days late pretty consistently, and I often have to remind him to invoice at all. This causes me to delay the billing cycle, which, as you can see, leads to a domino effect. I tried talking to him about it, but the issue has yet to be resolved. Do you have any ideas or suggestions on how to move forward?'

Again, collaborate! Be an ally. Don't make it into a big moral thing. It's just a workflow hiccup that can be fixed if everyone works together.

HOW TO DEAL WITH NASTY, RUDE, HORRIBLE, NO GOOD, VERY BAD COWORKERS

Over the course of your career, you're going to work with some people who need therapy. That's just the way it is. Your job is not to be their therapist. Your job is, quite literally, to learn how to work with them. So don't gossip, backstab, and/or try to get revenge. These things may seem fun and even deserved, but I promise that none of them will help you get to your desired outcome.

Instead, the first thing to try is what's called the Grey Rock Method. This is a technique that's used to avoid conflict with manipulative people. To 'Grey Rock' someone, you basically act as disinterested and disengaged as possible. It may not be as much fun as gossiping, but it is a whole lot more effective.

Most of the time, when someone is being rude, they're trying to get a rise out of you. It was true in kindergarten, and it's true now. This person wants you to get all angry and flustered so they can flip it on you and act like you're the rude one (ugh). Don't give them the satisfaction! Show no emotion, and only give one-word answers like, 'Yes', 'No', 'Sure', 'Thanks', 'Okay', etc. When they are denied the negative stimulus they crave, this person will most likely start to leave you alone.

If this doesn't work and this person continues being rude in a way that impedes your working relationship, I once again suggest getting them one-on-one. Remember, don't get mad; get curious. Try to learn from and about this person. It might be hard to accept, but if you were born into their situation and

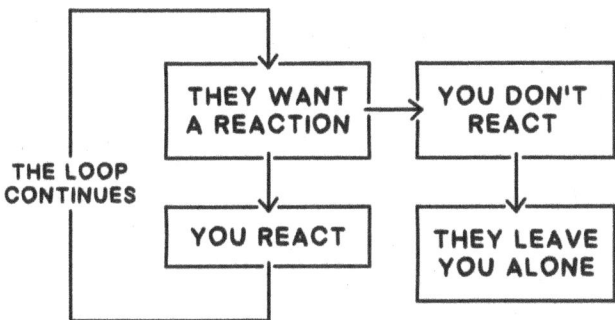

lived their life, you might act just like them. So try to find out what made them this way. Once again – empathy!

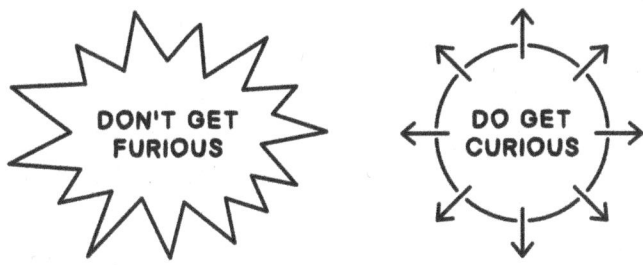

When talking to this person, don't say, 'What happened to you? Why are you like this?' Instead, ask about their previous work experience, what their current job is like, and what they do and don't enjoy about it. Most likely, they will reveal something that will give you at least a little bit of insight into their circumstances and what is driving their behaviour. Plus, people like it when others show interest in them. So even if nothing radical is revealed, hopefully this person will be friendlier to you going forward. And if not, hey, at least you tried.

WHAT TO DO WHEN A COWORKER IS FLIRTING OR ASKING YOU OUT

If a coworker is flirting or speaking to you suggestively, the obvious thing would be to run to report it to HR. My advice here is to set firm boundaries with soft words. Let this person know in a kind yet straightforward way that this is not okay with you, and it will not continue.

Try this: 'I know you're probably just joking around, but it makes me uncomfortable. Can you please only speak to me in a professional manner?' Then go report it to HR.

Now, if a coworker isn't flirting or being inappropriate per se but actually asks you on a date, your answer is extremely simple: 'Sorry, I don't date people I work with.' That's it. It's not a rejection, so you don't have to worry about the other person's bruised ego (not that you should really have to anyway . . .), but it is a firm boundary. Again, be soft with your words but firm with your boundaries.

And don't worry! If someone more attractive gets a job at your company, you can always change your mind and your policy. I kid, I kid!

WHAT TO DO WHEN A COWORKER LEAVES AND YOU GET STUCK WITH THEIR WORK

Typically, there are two times when you can get stuck with a coworker's tasks – when a coworker goes out on temporary leave (parental, sick or compassionate), or when a coworker quits or is let go and is not replaced right away. You might not like this, but if it's a short (one- to two-week) compassionate or sick leave, I recommend sucking it up and just helping your coworker out. Life happens, and most likely your coworker will end up doing you a favour at some point too. Be generous and helpful, and it'll come back around to you.

Now, if you get stuck with a coworker's tasks during a longer leave, that's a different story. In this case, the problem is not about you or your coworker. It's a reflection of a faulty system. Most good companies have policies in place so that this doesn't happen. If yours doesn't, have a conversation with your boss, but don't go in complaining about the extra work. Focus on the impact this will have on the company.

For example, say, 'I'm happy to help out while Lauren is on maternity leave, but I can't operate at my normal level of productivity while taking on these additional responsibilities. Does the company have a system in place to hire temp workers when people take leave?'

If your coworker is gone for good and the company is dragging its feet on replacing her, your conversation with your boss might be a tad more urgent. Don't say, 'I just think it's really unfair that after Max left you assumed that I'd automatically take on all his workload, and you didn't even give me a raise or title promotion or anything!'

Instead, go to your boss and say, 'I'd like to ask for your help. Since Max left and was not replaced, I've had to step up and take on the majority of his workload. While I'm willing to help out, this is unfortunately not a long-term solution for our team.'

In either case – a temporary or permanent leave – if your boss doesn't offer a solution, try this: 'We need to find a solution before we start running into workflow issues and losing clients. I've thought of two possible solutions. One, we hire a freelancer to take on Max's tasks until we can find a permanent solution. Two, I'm given an adjusted title and salary to reflect the work I'm currently doing. I think it's really important to find a solution within the next week, so thank you for making it a priority.'

Sticky Situations with Your Boss

It can be stressful to open up a potentially sticky conversation because of the inherent power dynamic. Of course, we don't like to be confrontational with our boss because we know they have the power to fire us. But remember that good bosses appreciate and foster open communication, and being assertive can make you more likeable. So don't be afraid to address issues with your boss in a professional manner. Here's how.

HOW TO TELL YOUR BOSS THAT YOU'RE OVERWORKED

Most of the time, when a boss asks you to do too many things at once, they aren't trying to overload you. They just don't realize how much you have on your plate. So how do you tell them this professionally? There is one key phrase here that will set you free: 'What would you like me to prioritize?'

For example, say your boss comes to you with a request: 'Hey, we just got a new script in. Can you read it and take notes by the end of the day?' But you're already working on something.

Should you just say yes because your boss asked, or say, 'Nope, sorry. Too busy!'? No. Instead, communicate your workload and ask your boss to pick a priority. 'Okay, I'm already working on a script breakdown, so do you think this one can wait until Monday, or would you like me to prioritize this new script over the one I'm currently working on?'

This is a straight line to your desired outcome (not having too much to do in one day or one week) because you're not complaining or taking extra work on. You're simply asking your boss to tell you what to focus on first.

WHAT TO DO WHEN YOUR BOSS IS A MICROMANAGER

A micromanager is a boss who overly monitors their employees' work. They may check in constantly, control your workflow and/or even step in and take over some of your tasks themselves. As annoying as this type of boss may be, before you start complaining or addressing it, you have to look in the mirror and honestly ask yourself if this is a Me ('Me' being you in this case) Problem.

Micromanaging tends to happen for one of two reasons – a lack of trust on the part of your boss or a lack of leadership skills. If your boss is micromanaging you because of a lack of trust, it's important to make sure you're not contributing to this dynamic.

Honestly, have you earned your boss's trust? Or have you been making mistakes or missing deadlines, causing your boss to lack confidence in your performance? If it's the latter, figure out what's causing you to have these issues and find a way to shape up. See if the micromanaging magically goes away once your boss learns to trust you.

If your performance has been stellar (be honest with yourself!) and your boss is still a micromanager, it's probably because they simply lack leadership skills and don't know how to properly delegate and manage employees. This means it is a You ('You' being your boss) Problem. My solution here is: Macromanage your boss so they stop micromanaging you. This basically comes down to preempting them with amazing communication. Get to them before they can get to you.

For example, if your boss typically messages you every morning at 9:00 asking for updates, make a habit of sending them an email at 8:30 saying, 'Here is an update on the progress I made yesterday and a list of my priorities for today.' Or you can try, 'I wanted to let you know that I'm getting started this morning on the project we discussed yesterday. I will check in with you before the end of the day to update you on my progress.' Hopefully, your boss will leave you alone to get your work done and learn to wait for your updates.

If this doesn't work or your boss is micromanaging on a particular project, try saying, 'I don't want you to have to keep checking in on me. It doesn't seem like the best use of your time. How about we set a meeting for tomorrow morning so I can show you my progress and you can give me feedback all at once?'

WHAT TO DO IF YOU'RE BUTTING HEADS WITH YOUR BOSS

Unfortunately, you're not always going to like your boss, and your boss isn't always going to like you. Or you might think that your boss doesn't like you, which may or may not be true. However, if you handle it well, none of this has to get in the way of your working relationship or your performance. Really.

The key here is to ask your boss for feedback. Maybe you're doing something that your old boss used to appreciate but that gets under this one's skin. Or maybe your boss just has a resting bitch face. Again, you'll never know if you don't ask. But don't just ask, 'Hey, you seem grumpy – is that just your face?' Instead, schedule a short one-on-one and say, 'I want to know if there's anything I can do to improve our working relationship. I want to make sure I'm the best account manager I can be, so please feel free to give me feedback and be blunt.'

If there is something specific that you think might be bothering your boss, ask for feedback on that too. But don't just say, 'Is this annoying you or what?' Try, 'My last boss really liked getting project reports each week, but I'm not sure if you find those useful. I'm happy to keep sending them if you do, but please feel free to let me know.'

If your boss insists that everything is fine, then you have to take her word for it. Assume that any grouchiness has nothing to do with you. Sure, there's a chance that she's being passive and isn't telling you the truth, but honestly, that's her problem. You've done all that you can do, and you have to just keep doing you!

HOW TO TELL YOUR BOSS THAT YOU'RE HAVING A BABY

Since the majority of people have children during their working years, deciding how to tell your boss that you're expecting is a common source of stress and anxiety. When do you tell them? How do you avoid being sidelined or overlooked for the good, juicy projects? How do you keep them from panicking and asking too many invasive questions?

It's important to know that you are in charge of when and how you share this information. Before you do, make sure to review your company's policies, which you can usually find in the company handbook. Educate yourself on the parental leave policies and any other programmes your company offers for coming back to work after your leave. Then decide when you want to share the news. Most women do it after the first trimester but before they're showing, but there's no law saying that you have to tell them then. (Partners – the same advice goes for you, since you'll likely be taking some parental leave too!)

When you're ready, sit down with your boss. Make sure you

have a tentative timeline mapped out and keep the conversation positive. If you appear confident and calm, your boss is more likely to be confident and calm too. Say:

'I wanted to share some good news – I'm expecting a baby this September. I know we have a lot going on, so I wanted to share my timeline with you. If all goes according to plan, I'll work until August 29. Right now, I plan on being on maternity leave until October 23. I have some ideas, but I wanted to get your input on the best ways to delegate my tasks. Oh, and I wanted to tell you early so we have time to prepare, but if you don't mind, I'd like to wait and tell the rest of the team myself.'

How to Handle Workplace Microaggressions and Other Inappropriate Behaviour

Some of the stickiest situations you may face at work are related to inappropriate or illegal behaviour. In the case of anything illegal or any sort of harassment, make sure to report it to HR, document everything in a safe place, and file a complaint to a government entity if necessary. If you believe illegal action has been taken towards you in the workplace, you should also feel free to reach out to an employment lawyer. If they think you have a case, they'll tell you. But hopefully this won't happen. You're more likely to face more subtle improprieties such as backhanded comments and microaggressions. Sigh.

Personally, I like to respond to microaggressions with laughter. This approach fits my personality and allows me to call out the behaviour without being flagged as problematic. For example, let's say a bunch of guys are standing around the office watercooler talking about investing. I walk up and say, 'What are you talking about?'

If their response is something subtly sexist like, 'Oh, we're just talking about complicated finance stuff,' I'll laugh and say something like, 'Ohhh, complicated finance stuff, gotcha!' or 'Is investing complicated? Hmm!' Adding a smile here is key. This way, I'm pointing out the ridiculousness of the comment without getting angry or defensive.

Another tactic that I love for responding to microaggressions is to repeat someone's words back to them but in a quizzical tone. For example, if someone says that you look tired, say to them curiously, 'I look tired?' Or if someone says that you look too young to be an attorney, say, 'I look too young to be an attorney?' Say no more, and let the awkwardness of their own words sink in. Then don't waste any more time on it and simply move on with the conversation.

If you want to add a little panache to this technique, try adding these two questions: 'Did you just say . . . ?' and 'Why would you say something like that?' For example, if someone points out that Gail doesn't have leadership potential, you can ask, 'Did you just say that Gail doesn't have leadership potential? Why would you say something like that?' Or you can try, 'Gail doesn't have leadership potential? Tell me more about that.'

If this person has a legitimate reason for their assertion, you're giving them a chance to share it. If not, they will have nothing to say. They'll be faced with their own nonsense comment, and you can leave it at that.

Sometimes, however, people continue saying inappropriate or offensive things despite your best efforts to defuse the situation. Again, if someone crosses the line, report it to HR. But what if they're bringing up something like politics in a way that makes everyone uncomfortable but isn't exactly illegal?

I would say that the first one or two times this happens, you should try to let it go. Don't jump to antagonizing the other person. Assume that they're just totally clueless and have no idea what they're saying. If it continues and is disruptive to your working relationship, try to nip it in the bud. Say, 'Would you mind if we just focus on the project? That would really help me concentrate.'

Unfortunately, much of the time these instances can be very subtle. For example, you're a woman and your boss is constantly asking you to grab the coffee, clean up the conference room or print the invitations, but never asks your male counterparts to do the same things. My strategy here is once again to set firm boundaries with soft words.

Maybe the first time this happens, you say, 'I can do it today, but next time let's find someone else to go so I can focus on preparing for the meeting.' If it keeps happening, you can kindly say no. Reinforce that boundary! Say, 'Sorry, I can't. I'm too busy preparing for the meeting.' You can even joke around and add in a bit of humour to defuse any tension, while still pointing out the mistreatment: 'I got the coffee last time. What gives? I think it's Tom's turn!' This way you can hint without being too confrontational.

Of course, as in any situation, it entirely depends on the context. In some instances, you might choose to say, 'I notice that you always ask me to do housekeeping tasks around the office, but rarely ask Tom or Jack. Why do you think that is?' Again, it's up to you. If you want to gently 'call them in' (I hate the phrase 'call them out' – it feels so superior to me!), then go for it. It's entirely up to you!

By the way, if you're the guy on the team, and you notice this happening (and you should pay attention), it would be super awesome of you to step up and offer to go instead. Say, 'Ana got the coffee for the last meeting. I'm happy to go this time.' The same thing goes any time you observe people acting from a place of bias. Speak up using any of the tactics above. You will be helping to make your workplace a happier, more inclusive environment, and that will benefit you and the people around you.

Feedback 101

Giving and receiving feedback at work doesn't have to be a sticky situation, but it often feels like one. If you're the one getting the feedback, it can be hard not to take it personally and get emotional. Then you feel embarrassed about getting emotional, and before you know it, you're in a full-blown spiral. If you're a manager and you're the one giving feedback, it can be equally stressful. You might worry about hurting the other person's feelings or them hating you or just worry that it's going to be really painful and awkward.

Well, it doesn't have to be! Giving and receiving feedback are normal parts of work culture. There's no avoiding it. These are skills that I want to challenge you to master.

HOW TO RECEIVE FEEDBACK WITHOUT CRYING

Like it or not, you are going to get a lot of feedback and even criticism in your life. Some of it is going to come from a good place from people who want to see you thrive. Some of it will come from a bad place from people who are just insecure or jealous.

To figure this out, I like to think of feedback as a baseball. Wait, hear me out. When your boss gives you feedback, imagine that she is throwing a baseball to you. Then you have a choice. You can let the ball hit you in the face, or you can lift up your mitt and catch it.

If you let the ball hit you, it's going to hurt. End of story. But if you catch the ball, you have a chance to take a look at it and ask yourself some questions. This is an internal script you can use in these moments: *Who threw this ball? Why did they throw it? Were they right to throw it? Should I take it home? If I take it home, should I put it on a shelf as a reminder? Or should I play with it and practise until I get better?*

Get it? The ball is the feedback. You're taking the time to consider the source, the context, and whether or not it's valid. Then you can decide how to engage with the ball or if you want to just drop it and move on with your day. But either way, don't let the baseball hit you in the face!

While you're having this internal conversation, your external script should be extremely simple: 'Thank you for the feedback. I will absolutely take that into consideration going forward.' Use this regardless of how valid the feedback is or isn't.

Say your boss says, 'I noticed that you are more than five

minutes late to the majority of meetings. This may seem like a small thing, but it's really important to be on time, especially for client meetings. Is this something you can work on?'

Don't: 'Why do you hate me?'

Don't: 'I am NOT late to every meeting, and half the time we end up waiting for the client, anyway. So I don't understand why you're nitpicking the tiniest thing when literally no one cares.'

Do: 'Thank you for the feedback. I will absolutely take that into consideration going forward.'

Or, if your boss says, 'I've noticed that there have consistently been typos in the annual reports that you write. These go to senior management, so it's really important that they're proofread and polished before you send them out.'

Don't: 'Those aren't even typos – it's not my fault that you don't know grammar!'

Don't: 'Ugh, who cares? I bet none of those crusty old dudes even read them!'

Do: 'Thank you for the feedback. I will take that into consideration going forward.'

You get it.

HOW TO GIVE FEEDBACK WITHOUT MAKING THE OTHER PERSON CRY

If you're early in your career, you might not be in a position to give feedback to others just yet, but as you progress, it's more than likely that one day you will be. Giving effective feedback is an art, and it's an incredibly important part of being a manager. So it's worth learning and perfecting this skill now, assuming that you'll be the boss one day.

I must admit that my opinion on the best way to give feedback has really changed over the years. I used to be a big fan of the 'Oreo Method', which is basically a feedback sandwich with compliments as the bread. In other words, you give the feedback in this order: compliment, feedback, compliment.

For example: 'Overall, this has been your best year yet. You're really stepping up to the plate and taking on new projects, and I'm impressed. There's one piece of advice I want to give you, which is to work on active listening, especially in meetings. This is a really important skill, and it's something that I want to challenge you to master in the coming year. I've noticed that you do a great job of articulating your own ideas in meetings, though, so kudos on that.'

There's nothing wrong with this method, but as I've progressed in my own career, I've found that it's more effective to be even more straightforward when giving feedback. As the recipient of feedback, I've grown the most from the feedback that stung in the moment. So, my best advice is to rip off that Band-Aid. This goes for giving feedback or any sort of bad news. Don't just blurt out, 'Stop interrupting people in meetings!' Instead, use this four-step process:

1. Frame the conversation and ask if this is a good time. This prepares the other person to hear bad news and ensures that they have consented to hearing it. You can say, 'Hey, is now a good time? I have a quick piece of feedback I wanted to share with you.'
2. Once they've agreed to hear the news, get right to it. For example, 'I've noticed that you're interrupting people a lot in meetings.' Boom. Band-Aid OFF.
3. Now soften the blow and provide more context. For example, 'I really appreciate how enthusiastic you are. You honestly have great ideas. However, it makes it difficult for people to listen to your ideas when you're interrupting.'
4. Finally, ask if they have any questions about the feedback. You can literally just ask, 'Do you have any questions about this?'

Whichever method you choose, at the end of the day, giving feedback is all about expressing the fact that this person is already doing a good job, and if they tweak this one thing, they'll be even better. And most important, that you are on their side and want to help them.

OF COURSE, your workplace, your coworkers and your boss will present their own unique forms of sticky, uncomfortable

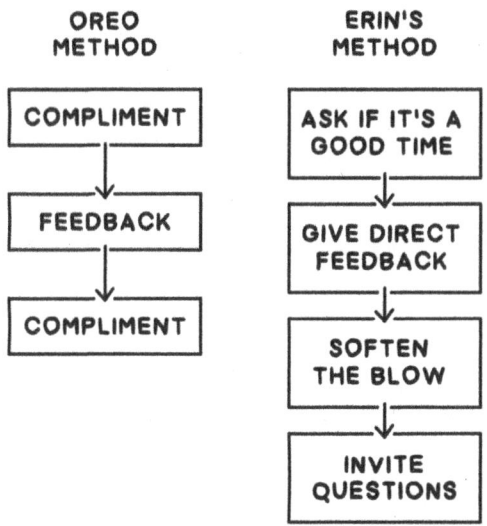

situations. But you should be able to riff on the scripts and techniques above to unstick them so these issues start to roll right off your back. And now that you have learned pretty much everything there is to know about how to land a job and thrive in your career, let's wrap up with the last thing you'll do at nearly every job you have – quit!

CHAPTER 10

How to Quit Your Job Gracefully

We must be willing to let go of the life we've planned, so as to have the life that is waiting for us.

—JOSEPH CAMPBELL

First impressions? They're overrated. In his book *Never Split the Difference*, Chris Voss writes, 'The last impression is the lasting impression.' While most folks focus on how 'you don't get a second chance at a first impression', you can get over a mediocre first impression. It's the last impression that truly sticks with people.

So how you leave a job matters just as much as how you start a job. It can feel so tempting to say, 'I QUIT! I hate it here, you are the worst boss on earth, this is the most toxic workplace ever, and I hope I never see you again!!!' It's unfortunately a short-lived high though. You need to squash this urge and rise above it.

Now, don't get me wrong, I am 100 per cent a fan of you expressing your anger and airing your grievances. It's not healthy to keep things in; I don't want you to explode. But do it in a way that is smart and that benefits you! I don't care about your boss, HR, or your coworkers' feelings. I care about you, so my advice is what's in your best interest long term. It's important to remember that after you leave a job, your reputation lies with the people you left there.

In the 1988 film *Working Girl* (great movie), Sigourney Weaver's character teaches an important lesson to her secretary, 'Never burn bridges. Today's junior [jerk], tomorrow's senior partner.' We tend to think the people around us are frozen in time and that they will stay in their job forever. But the reality, especially these days, is that people will change roles and companies many times, just like you.

There is a solid chance you will run into the people you knew at earlier jobs again later on. Who knows? Maybe you log in to a Zoom call for a potential new client, and it's the wife of your incompetent, crusty old boss. That old manager you ghosted and left hanging? Surprise! Their kid goes to school with your kid – and they're a manager at a company you'd die to get an interview with. The world is much, much smaller than you think, and trust me, people talk. If you won't listen to me, listen to Sigourney – you never know where someone is going to end up. Instead, give everyone a reason to remember you fondly. I'm going to show you how.

Why Quitting Can Be Hard

Quitting your job can feel surprisingly stressful and emotional. Even if it's something you want to do, leaving a job can come with a lot of mixed emotions. You might feel guilty letting your boss down (especially if they were a pretty good boss), leaving your coworkers behind, or abandoning your clients. You might feel strangely sad or incredibly relieved, or you might be straight-up excited. Or maybe you feel everything, everywhere, all at once!

I want you to know that all of that is completely normal. We spend the majority of our waking hours working, so when you change up when and where and with whom you work every day, it can feel monumental. Many of us also have our identities wrapped up in what we do, so this shift can feel like a lot. Change, even good change, can be very hard. But remember: Just because you're sad doesn't make it the wrong decision. You can be sad about a decision, and it can still 100 per cent be the right thing to do.

It's okay for a lot of emotions to come up. Take some time to process them, and do what you've got to do. But I'll say it about a gazillion more times – it's not personal; it's just professional. You're not dying. You're just moving on to another job. Your boss has had people quit on them before, and they'll have people quit on them again. Onboarding and offboarding people are part of their job description as a manager, so don't waste your energy feeling guilty. Any good boss will be happy that you're moving on. And the lame bosses? The ones who get angry, act 'surprised', say passive-aggressive comments, insist on details, or beg you to stay? Don't worry, we'll get to all that.

It is important, however, that you do this right in order to protect yourself from things getting messy. Part of the hidden curriculum is knowing the right way to walk away. There are specific steps you need to take. And keep in mind that laws around quitting your job vary from country to country. Some countries have strict policies about giving notice. In the US, for example, you can technically pick up and leave the same day (in 99 per cent of cases). It is customary but not mandatory to give two weeks' notice. So, with that said, let's dive into quitting your job and moving on to bigger and better things!

How Not to Quit a Job

First, let's look at the wrong way to quit a job. Take Lisa, who has been at her job at a nonprofit for four years and has been looking to move on for nine months or so. While she enjoyed her job at first, she has grown frustrated with the lack of upward mobility and false promises regarding raises.

After a fairly lengthy job search, Lisa lands a great offer with another nonprofit. Lisa is pumped. She updates her coworkers, whom she's kept looped in on her job search, and books a vacation. She plans to tell her boss that she's quitting on Friday.

Well, on Wednesday, Lisa's boss asks her to hop on a quick Zoom call and says, 'Is it true that you're leaving?'

'Oh, yeah, I was going to tell you on Friday,' Lisa replies sheepishly.

'Well, no need to,' her boss says curtly. 'Today is your last day. We will mail out your last paycheque. Best of luck to you in whatever you're doing next.'

Lisa's years of repressed anger come up to the surface. She blurts out, 'How dare you!? I have been nothing but good to you as you've treated all of us like crap the past few years. You're just another rich housewife running a broken nonprofit to make herself feel better and probably avoid taxes ... or something! I'm done with you; I never want to see you again!' Lisa slams her laptop shut.

The next day, Lisa receives an email from her new job asking if she can push the start date back a few months. They're saying that Q2 is when they will have the budget to start her role, and she'll have to wait until then to get onboarded. Here Lisa is: unemployed, standing among burned bridges and bad karma. At least she has a vacation booked?

All right, let's talk about some key mistakes Lisa made. First, she talked about her job search with her current coworkers. This is a bad move for several reasons, but the most important is discretion – aka your coworkers are blabbermouths. Save your job-search news for your personal friends and family. Expect everything you tell a coworker to get out at work. Gossip is prevalent, and people are bored. I'm sorry to be so cynical, but it's the truth!

Second, Lisa quit before she had a formally signed offer with her new organization, which is a rookie mistake. You should always have a completed, signed contract with your new job before quitting your old job. It's okay to keep working your current job as normal, because until it's signed, you never know for sure if the new offer is going to go through.

In the United States, an employer can terminate for any legal reason at any time. This means that when an employee puts in their two weeks' notice, they should be prepared for them to say, 'You know what? I don't want you sticking around here for two weeks. Today is your last day – see ya!' Now, most employers will not do this, but toxic/unprofessional companies still exist, and this does still happen. Companies do not like dead men/women walking.

Third, and most detrimental, Lisa went off on her boss. She completely blew up, unleashing years of repressed anger and bitterness. You may be wondering, *What's so bad about that, Erin? It sounds like her boss was horrible.* Exactly. Her boss is horrible. And she just gave her ammo to be more horrible.

Seriously, do you think that telling someone off is going to give them a wake-up call? A change of heart? A moment of clarity? Heck no. It's going to enrage them. When your next prospective employer calls your previous boss for a reference, this gives them the perfect opportunity to say negative things about you. And before you say that a previous boss can't give you a bad recommendation . . . Yeah, that's not the case. There is almost no way to monitor reference checks. Prospective employers will contact previous employers, and they'll have a chat that no one else listens in on.

While you can't control what is said during these checks, you can control how you leave your previous role. Blowing up and telling people off is simply not in your best interest. It feels good in the moment, but that feeling is fleeting and will follow you as a dark cloud for the rest of your life. I know, sometimes my advice isn't sexy and fun – but it is realistic!

The good news is that there are plenty of healthy ways to express your anger and frustration. For starters, Glassdoor.co.uk is a fantastic platform where you can anonymously express feelings toward a previous or current employer, warning others who are curious about working there. Fishbowl and Reddit are other great platforms. You can also journal or write a letter saying all the things you bite your tongue on and throw it into a roaring fire for dramatic effect.

You can go to therapy, or ask a friend if you can vent. You can scream into a pillow, start kickboxing, or the best revenge of all, live a happy and healthy life where you don't give your toxic boss/old job a second thought. It's not your job to fix your old company. You worked there, and now you don't! Simple as that.

You can, of course, request an exit interview if you would like to give feedback to the company. But remember, feedback is a way of showing you care, so if you don't care about the company, there is no need to do this. If you do choose to do an exit interview, there are plenty of ways to say, 'Eff you', but in corporate.

For example, if HR asks you for any feedback regarding your toxic boss, you might blabber: 'I'm sorry, but they are literally the most mentally deranged, controlling, terrible boss I've ever had!' Instead, you could try something a bit more stealth and professional, like, 'I believe my previous boss would benefit from extensive leadership training, as their management methods were inefficient and often counterintuitive.' This way, you aren't responsible for shit talking, but you are offering genuine, tangible feedback that HR can document. It's not personal, just professional, remember?

The Quitting Order of Operations

While quitting can feel overwhelming, I've broken this process down to six simple steps that will help you do it professionally with confidence and ease. Here we go:

Step 1: You may be eager to rip off the Band-Aid, but I am literally begging you not to jump the gun and quit too early. Wait until you have your new job offer signed, sealed and delivered. I don't care if you're a shoo-in for a new job or even if you've already got an offer! Technically, until that offer letter is signed, anything can happen. The last thing you want is to have to go back to your boss with your tail between your legs and beg for your old job back. That's not a good look, you know?

And while I'm on this subject, before you land a new job, don't tell or even imply to your boss that you're out there looking. You may think this will make them try to entice you to stay, but it's more likely to backfire. Once your boss knows that you have one foot out the door, they're not motivated to support your growth. They know you're just biding your time until a new offer comes along. Keep it classy, keep it professional, and keep it to yourself until the time is right.

Step 2: Check your employment contract for the correct notice period and work it out from there. This notice period applies to your employer as well as you, the employee.

Assuming your notice period is two weeks, this will allow you to spend some time . . . in the lurch. However, it could be one week or one month, so work with the timings accordingly.

If you're leaving a toxic workplace or just really want time to take a vacation before starting your new job, you can work that into your notice period. If you haven't used your holiday quota, you can take that before your leaving date if you really have to get out, or you can work right up to that date and receive holiday pay in your final paycheque.

Step 3: This is the big moment. But don't just walk up to your boss and say, 'I quit!' First, schedule a brief meeting. Say to your boss, 'Hey, can I put a fifteen-minute meeting on your calendar?' Choose a Monday or Friday, depending on your last day. It's likely that they'll assume correctly what this meeting is about. Like I said, they've had people quit on them before. This is a good thing because it means they'll be prepared.

It's important that you don't tell anyone else at work that you're leaving before this meeting with your boss. Look at what happened to Lisa. News can spread around a workplace really fast, and you definitely want your boss to hear it from you first.

When the meeting comes around, you are going to verbally give your notice. Keep this conversation authentic, professional and to the point. For the sake of all bosses everywhere, please do not dance around it. Now is the time to rip the Band-Aid off! Here's a sample script:

'Hi Brian, thanks for sitting down with me. I'll cut right to the chase. I have accepted an offer at another company and will be putting in my two weeks' notice today. So, my last day will be Friday the fourteenth. I've enjoyed my time here and am grateful for the opportunities I've had, but it feels like the right time for me to move on.'

Now, your boss is going to respond in one of a few possible ways. A good boss will probably say something like, 'Oh no, that's what I suspected. We hate to lose you, but I'm so glad to hear you found an opportunity you're excited about.'

However, a toxic boss might try to guilt trip you by saying something like, 'What? You're completely blindsiding me! How can you leave when we're so busy and already barely getting by?'

If this happens, remember, this is not a Me Problem. This is a You Problem. Don't fall for it and say, 'Okay fine, I'll stay.' But also, don't fire back, 'Are you freaking kidding me?! How is that my problem? Learn how to run a company, this isn't my fault!'

Do the best you can to ignore the guilt trip and go with grace. Say something like, 'I understand, but I'm sure you'll be able to find someone in no time. And as I said, I'm more than happy to stay for two weeks to help with the transition.' Then move on. This person doesn't care about you, so don't waste any emotional energy worrying about them.

The third possible way for your boss to respond is by making you a counteroffer. They might say something like, 'Oh no – is there anything I can do to convince you to stay? Name your number, and I'll take it to HR.' This may be tempting in the moment, but I'd say that about 90 per cent of the time it's not worth considering.

Think about it this way: If you've gone through all this work to find a new job, there's a reason you're leaving, and it's probably not just money. If, and only if, the company, your boss, the clients, the coworkers, and literally every single thing about your current job is great except for the pay, then it might be worth considering their counter.

Most likely, though, there are reasons you're leaving besides money. If that's the case, don't even entertain a counteroffer. Just get out of there. You can say, 'Thank you so much. That's so generous. But it feels like the right time for me to move on.'

Regardless of how your boss responds, if they ask you questions about where you're going or why, it's completely up to you to decide if you want to tell them. This is based on your comfort level and your comfort level alone.

You can be vague and say something like, 'Oh, I'm going to another tech company,' or 'I've felt that the culture here hasn't been great lately, and I'm looking for a healthier work dynamic,' or 'I've been offered a role with greater responsibilities, and it seems like a great next step for my career.' Again, keep it professional. Be honest, but don't vent or throw a tantrum. Your desired outcome is to leave on a positive and authentic note, so focus on that.

Step 4: Make it official and draft a resignation letter. In general, it's always a good idea to have things in writing. You can keep this really simple. For example:

Dear Boss,

Thanks for sitting down with me. To confirm, I gave my two weeks' notice today, and my last day at the company will be June 14. Thank you for this opportunity and I wish you the best of luck.

Sincerely,

Erin

If you really liked working with your boss, feel free to personalize this message. Add in some gratitude and appreciation. This can go a long way.

Step 5: Tie up loose ends with coworkers. Typically, your boss will announce to the team that you're leaving, so don't immediately go spreading the news. Once the announcement has been made, it's a good idea to reach out to colleagues to ask for their personal contact info and/or to connect with them on LinkedIn. These people are an important part of your network. Remember, they'll move on too. Also consider whether you want to ask anyone at the company for a letter of recommendation. It'll probably be easier to get this now than in a year or two when they barely remember you (no offence – I'm sure you're super memorable).

Not sure how to ask? Try this:

'Hi Paula! I've really enjoyed working with you these past three years. I know we've been able to accomplish a lot together, and I'm wondering if you'd be willing to write me a short recommendation on LinkedIn. If you're not comfortable doing that or can't right now, that's completely fine. I thought I'd ask because I respect you as a colleague and a recommendation from you would carry a lot of weight. Thank you!' This is especially great to do if you were laid off or don't have your next employment lined up quite yet.

Finally, collect any work you've done that you can include in your portfolio. Basically, think about anything that would be useful to have once you no longer have access to your work email, files, etc. and send them to your personal email or make hard copies. (Make sure this is all within legal limits, of course!)

Step 6: Depending on the company, you might have to have another meeting with HR to tie up any loose ends or complete necessary paperwork, and many companies do conduct standard exit interviews. The irony is that usually the most well-run companies offer exit interviews and the toxic ones do not, but you can always request one. As I mentioned before, this is your time to professionally provide feedback about why you're leaving and hopefully make an impact on the company. You can also ask your soon-to-be-former boss if they would like to receive feedback from you.

If your boss and/or HR do ask for feedback, remember to keep it light and professional. Instead of saying, 'Yeah, my boss was kinda psycho, and that's why I'm leaving, TBH,' try something like, 'While I enjoyed my team and coworkers, the management I operated under is ultimately the reason for my leaving. I found my direct supervisor's leadership style to be abrasive, curt and sometimes cruel. This made it hard for me to do my job, and despite attempts to improve our working relationship, it has resulted in my needing to find a new role. I wish this wasn't the case and that my boss was receptive to feedback. But I wanted to share this frank critique with you in the hopes of improving the company and providing context for my leaving.'

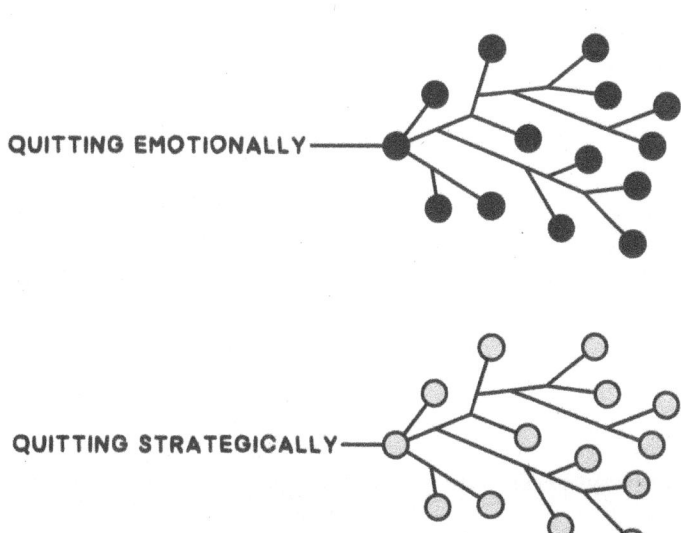

WELL, LOOK AT that. You've successfully and professionally quit your job to move on to bigger and brighter things. Remember to leave on a good note, even when it's hard. This job feels like your entire life right now, but soon, it'll just be a memory. It's now a part of your story, and no matter what, it's good for the plot. Everything is a learning experience. Keep discovering what you love and what you hate, and carry that awareness into every role you take on.

CONCLUSION

Words Are Powerful

I hope that by now I've convinced you of the incredible impact that strong, professional communication can have not just on your career, but on the rest of your life. The communication skills you've learned in this book are now a permanent part of your tool kit, and here's the best part: No one can ever take them from you. These tools are yours to keep, sharpen and use as often as you need – and trust me, you will need them.

I'm guessing that before you even cracked open this book, you already had a clear idea of *what* you wanted, but you didn't know *how* to get it. You knew you wanted to land that great new job, negotiate a raise without feeling awkward, or finally set boundaries with your overly demanding boss. But like so many others, you probably felt stuck in the gap between the 'what' and the 'how'. You're not alone.

The amazing thing is that now you know how. You've closed that gap. So I want you to pause for a moment and revisit your 'what'. Think back to why you picked up this book in the first place. Was it to prepare for a big job interview? To deal with a difficult coworker? Or maybe just to arm yourself with a new sense of confidence when communicating?

With that 'what' in mind, I challenge you to put these skills into action *today*. Don't wait for the perfect moment – it's never coming. Take the leap. Send that cold email to the leader in your industry you admire. Schedule a one-on-one with your boss to share your goals for the year and ask for support in achieving them. Sit down with that coworker you used to get along with but who's been giving you major side-eye lately.

You know what you want, and now you know how to ask for it. So don't overthink it – take a deep breath, listen to your mum's advice, and *use your words*. Chances are, this will help you get closer to your desired outcome. But even if it doesn't work immediately, I guarantee you'll feel a million times better just for taking action. And here's the magic of it: The more you have these conversations, the easier they'll become. Professional communication is a muscle – start flexing it now, and let me know how it goes. I genuinely can't wait to hear about it!

But before I wrap this up, I have two more things I want you to do. (I know, I'm so demanding. Stay with me.) First, pass this knowledge on to someone else. Share these tools with a friend, coworker or mentee. Let's work together to make the hidden curriculum more visible and accessible to everyone. Empowering others isn't just the right thing to do – it also makes workplaces better for all of us. The more people who know how to communicate professionally, the less stress, drama and unnecessary tension we all have to deal with.

Second, don't forget to have good, healthy conversations with *yourself*. You can use every script in this book, but if your inner dialogue is abusive, belittling or overly critical, it will hold you back. Be your own supportive, honest and loving best friend. Speak to yourself with the same kindness and encouragement you'd offer to someone you love.

On that note, I'll leave you with a favourite quote commonly attributed to my girl Eleanor Roosevelt: 'No one can make you feel inferior without your consent.' As you step into these powerful conversations, *recklessly believe in yourself.* Don't let anyone make you feel small, and don't give away your power. Keep your eyes glued on that desired outcome. Your words are yours to wield. They're your superpower, and no one can take them from you.

Say it loudly to yourself (in your head if you're in public, please):

'I'm going to land my dream job.'

'I'm going to become the CEO of my own company.'

'I'm going to have a one-million-dollar net worth by the time I'm forty.'

Be bold, be confident, and yes, even a little delusional. (But, you know, not *Elizabeth Holmes–level* delusional – stay ethical, folks.)

Here's the truth: You are worthy of all the things you want. Your dream life is out there waiting for you, and it's begging you to hurry up already. You have all the tools you need to make it happen. Something incredible is right around the corner – I can feel it in my bones! Go out there, take this world by storm, and please, let me know what you accomplish. I'll be cheering for you every step of the way. You got this!

ACKNOWLEDGEMENTS

While this book may have my name on it, it's truly the result of so many individuals' hard work behind the scenes. Every titbit of advice, every nugget of wisdom in this book was inspired by someone I've met along the way. So to all the people who have whispered advice to me, passing down the hidden rules and secret language of work: thank you. In addition to inspiration, there was also a small army of people who got this book over the finish line, into print and available for you to read. Let me tell you about them.

First, I want to thank my editor, Megan McCormack, and her meticulous and passionate team at Portfolio/Penguin for believing in me and this book since day one. Thank you, Megan, for saying my name in a room of possibility and offering your graceful direction to whip this first-time author into shape. I also would like to thank Adrian Zackheim, Niki Papadopoulos, Margot Stamas, Brian Borchard, Lucile Culver, Jacquelyn Gilando, and all other hands at Portfolio who touched this book.

To my sharp-as-a-tack agent, Samantha Schmidt, and her wonderful team at Gersh Digital for supporting me in all my endeavours (and to our friend Alyssa Joseph for bringing us together). Thank you, Sam, for answering my 'Hey, I got an email from a publisher . . . how do I do this?' text. Remember, kids, no one knows what they're doing. Except Sam. I think she might know.

To my literary agent, David Doerrer, for walking me through the secret language of 'how to sell a book'. Your strategy, poise and dedication to this book was and still is greatly appreciated. To my assistant-turned-friend Tatiana Rincon, for providing endless support and being employee No. 1, and everyone who has worked on the AdviceWithErin team over the years. To Janis Ozolins, for taking these words and illustrating them to help my fellow visual learners.

To my incisive, perceptive and tenacious writing partner, Jodi Lipper, for keeping me on track, steering me, challenging me and slowly reeling me back in after letting me go on interesting albeit completely irrelevant tangents. Your work ethic, dedication to your craft and persistence taught me to so much.

To my siblings, the smartest people I know – thank you for all the late-night debates, book and podcast recommendations, and always keeping me humble (I forgive you for mac-n-cheese-hot-sauce gate). I'm so happy to be a member of your tribe.

To my extended family, aunts, uncles, cousins, nieces, nephews and wonderful in-laws for reminding me that the best way to connect with others is through laughter. We are our village – and I don't take mine for granted. I love my silly, wine-lovin', creek-sittin', crab-pickin' folk. Never change.

To my business mentors and partners throughout the years – this book is a collection of greatest hits I learned from you.

Thank you. To Adam Loria and Sophie Bressler at Night Media. Your savviness, tenacity and drive are amazing to witness (and even more amazing to work with). Thank you for supporting this book and the AdviceWithErin mission as a whole.

To my stunning, hilarious, inspiring girlfriends. You are my greatest role models. Don't you just love it when women?

To anyone who said I was too ambitious, or I was too young, or I was too green, or I just needed to be 'more realistic' – thank you. Seriously! Spite is a really fantastic motivator for me. And I got to use that motivation to write a whole book empowering people to follow their dreams. Funny how that works.

To my parents and fellow writers, Chris and Claire, for encouraging me to go out and 'dent the universe'. To my dad, for constantly telling me I was 'born a leader' for as long as I can remember – thanks for teaching me how to bet on myself and never make excuses. Oh, and for the thirty years of career advice! None of this would exist without your wisdom. To my mum, for teaching me how to keep two feet on the ground, listen to my intuition and kill them with kindness. Your poetry isn't just in your writing, but also in how you live. Thank you both for showing me the power my words have and for leading by example.

To my dog, Olive – my soul dog – for lying under my desk, staying up as late as I needed, with no complaints, as I typed away. The unconditional love and loyalty of all dogs is something I hope no one takes for granted.

And finally, to Michael, my husband – a boy I met in high school and have been obsessed with ever since. I am in constant awe of your talent, dedication and care in all that you do. Every day, you inspire me to be a better person. No one has had to hear more about this book than Michael (he can probably recite it from memory). Thank you for always making sure I have enough water and sunlight, and for always being there for me, ever since my rough draft.

NOTES

1. Allan and Barbara Pease, 'The Definitive Book of Body Language', *New York Times*, September 24, 2006.

2. Jodi Schulz, 'Eye Contact: Don't Make These Mistakes', Michigan State University, MSU Extension, December 31, 2012, https://www.canr.msu.edu/news/eye_contact_dont_make_these_mistakes.

3. Lou Adler, 'New Survey Reveals 85% of All Jobs Are Filled Via Networking', LinkedIn.com, February 29, 2016, https://www.linkedin.com/pulse/new-survey-reveals-85-all-jobs-filled-via-networking-lou-adler/.

4. N. Epley and J. Schroeder, 'Mistakenly Seeking Solitude,' *Journal of Experimental Psychology: General* 143, no. 5 (2014): 1980–99, https://doi.org/10.1037/a0037323; Neha Bose and Daniel Sgroi, 'The Role of Personality Beliefs and "Small Talk" in Strategic Behaviour', *PLOS One* (September 2, 2022), https://doi.org/10.1371/journal.pone.0269523.

5. 'Work Smart & Start Smart: Salary Negotiation', American Association of University Women, https://www.aauw.org/resources/programs/salary-negotiation.

6. Jeff Haden, 'Research Shows Not Negotiating Your Salary Could Cost You $1 Million (Especially Women)', *Inc.*, December 19, 2016, https://www.inc.com/jeff-haden/research-shows-not-negotiating-your-salary-could-cost-you-1-million-especially-.html.

7. Alison Wood Brooks, 'Emotion and the Art of Negotiation', *Harvard Business Review*, December 2015.

8. Jena McGregor, 'Asking for a Bigger Starting Salary Pays Off Most of the Time: Survey', *Forbes*, April 5, 2023.

9. Alyssa Pomponio and Amanda Elkins, 'Negotiation in the Workplace', Well-Being at Iowa, University of Iowa, December 7, 2023.

INDEX

accomplishments, visibility of, 193–95
Adlerian psychology, 30–31
advocating, for self
  in asking for promotion, 189–91
  with bosses, 187–89
  lack of, 183–85
  saying 'no' in, 186–87
  visibility of accomplishments in, 193–95
affiliate groups, 78–79
aggressive communication. *See also* passive-aggressive communication
  authentic alternative to, 12
  defining, 38
  examples of, 38, 39–40
  hypermasculine, 11–12, 147
  negotiations and, 147
  self-reflection about, 39
AI (artificial intelligence) help, 102, 145
Angelou, Maya, 51
anger

conversation type misunderstanding and, 33
  quitting job and, 226–27, 229–30, 231
  rude coworkers and, 208–9
  self-awareness around, 19–20
anxiety
  interview, 99–103, 109–10
  mental, 101–2
  physiological, 101
  self-esteem issues and, 102–3
articulate speech
  overtalking impact on, 28–29
  'sandwich' thoughts relation to, 26
  tips for learning, 24
artificial intelligence (AI) help, 102, 145
assertive communication
  advocating for self and, 185
  with coworkers interrupting, 192–93
  defining, 38
  examples, 39–40

assertive communication (*cont.*)
   as goal, 38–39
   self-reflection about, 39
authenticity
   email sign-off and, 58–59
   filler words and, 41
   negotiations and, 148
   in professional communication, 9–13
   in quitting job, 236–37

backward-facing language, 46–48
best interests
   communication matching, 10
   of company, 127–28
   emotional outbursts negating, 231
   protecting your, 181, 227
   rejection response and, 67
BLUF ('Bottom Line Up Front'), 60–61
body language
   eye contact, 49–50
   foundational tips for mastering, 49–53
   hand gestures, 50
   in interviews, 108–9
   mirroring, 51–52
   observation of, 25
   posture, 51, 109
   research findings on, 48, 49
   smiles, 50–51
bosses
   advocating for self with, 187–89
   approaching for a raise, 43–44, 144–45, 156–59
   bait and switch with new, 203–4
   boundary setting with, 174–76
   conflicts with, 215–16
   expectation clarity with, 170–72
   factual/change conversation with, 34, 37
   feedback from, 172, 214, 215, 221–22
   feedback to HR about, 232, 238–40
   interview questions about former, 117–18, 127–28
   lazy coworker behaviour told to, 205–6, 207
   Me Problem / You Problem discernment with, 29–32, 213, 214
   micromanaging behaviour from, 213–15
   new job expectations set with, 168–72
   new job feedback request of, 172
   new job relationship building with, 166
   new job search kept from current, 233
   overwhelm communicated with, 29–30, 31, 38, 212–13
   passive-aggressive communication from, 38, 216
   positive language with, 46
   pregnancy communicated to, 216–17
   promotion discussion with, 189–91
   quitting job meeting with, 234–35

quitting job response from,
    229–30, 235–36
renegotiating current salary
    with, 144–45
sticky situations with, 196–97,
    212–17
underpromising and
    overdelivering approach
    with, 168–70
visibility of accomplishments
    with, 193–95
workload issues communication
    with, 211–13
'Bottom Line Up Front' (BLUF),
    60–61
boundaries
  after-hours emails and,
      171–72
  with bosses, 174–76
  with clients, 180–81
  with coworkers, 178,
      179–80, 210
  freelance work, 180–81
  microaggressions and, 219
  new job, 168–72
  overdelivering and erosion of,
      162–63
  positive language for setting, 46
  relationship-building caution
      with, 174–76, 179
  setting and reinforcing, 13, 46,
      173–82
  sustainable workload and,
      162–63
breathwork, 109–10
Brown, Brené, 1, 39
'but,' word swap for, 43–44

Campbell, Joseph, 226
Captivate (Van Edwards), 50
career success
  advocating for self and, 183–85
  networking key to, 69–70
  positive attitude key for, 45, 102
  self-talk impact on, 102
  spectrum of, 8
  uncomfortable conversations
      and, 135–36
changes, small
  big impacts from, examples of,
      23–29
  power of, 17, 18
chess metaphor, 7–8, 10
clients
  boundary setting with, 180–81
  honesty role in trust from, 127
  sticky situation in billing,
      196–97
closed-ended questions, 44–45
clothing
  conversation pieces and,
      93–94
  interview, 104–5
communication styles
  emotions triggered with,
      19–21, 39
  overview, 37–38
  using correct, 37–40
compensation packages
  negotiating, 155, 159–60
  salary flexibility with, 120,
      154, 155
competence, 147–48
competitive approach, 171
  promotions and, 193–94

confidence, 243
  external validation relation to, 21–22
  interviewing and, 101–3, 109–10, 119
  mindset, 21–23
  negative self-talk impact on, 22–23
  negotiating demonstrating, 140
  posture impacting, 51, 109
conflicts. *See also* sticky situations
  with bosses, 215–16
  conversation type misunderstanding and, 32–34
  forward-facing language with, 47
  Grey Rock Method for, 208
  interview questions about handling, 126, 127–28
  Me Problem / You Problem discernment in, 29–32, 235
  opponent into ally in, 206–7
  passive-aggressive communication in, 37–38
  people pleasing and, 30–31
connection. *See also* networking
  elevator pitch for making, 85–86
  hidden job market, 70–72
  interest and curiosity role in making, 92–93
  open-ended questions and opportunities for, 44–45
  quitting and considering future, 227
  reciprocity principle value in, 73, 80–81
  shared interests and creating, 78–79
  verbal mirroring for, 52–53, 153
  warm outreach online for established, 76–79
conversation pieces, 93–94
conversation starters
  with new coworkers, 165, 167–68
  PAGE for, 91–92
  small talk tips and, 87–90
conversation types, 32–37
The Courage to Be Disliked (Kishimi and Koga), 30–31
Covey, Stephen, 6
coworkers
  boundary setting with, 178, 179–80, 210
  conversation starters with new, 165, 167–68
  conversation style examples with, 39–40
  conversation type match between, 34, 35–36
  conversation type misunderstanding, 32–34
  flirting, 210
  interruptions from, 191–93
  lazy or unprofessional, 204–7
  quitting job and telling, 234–35, 237–38
  relationship building with, 164–65, 167–68
  rude, 208–9
  self-awareness of reactions to, 19–20
  small talk with, 88–90

INDEX

staying connected with, 237–38
sticky situations with, 204–12
word and phrasing swaps with, 42–48
workload from absent, 210–12
Cuban, Mark, 99
Cuddy, Amy, 147
curiosity, 92–93
   interview questions demonstrating, 131–32

desired outcome
   clarity around, 3, 6, 241–42
   envisioning, 6, 243
   strategic communication for, 6–7, 242
discrimination, 123–25
disrespect, 177–78
documentation
   new job and, 166–67
   quitting job and, 232, 238–39
drama, workplace, 174, 179–80, 208, 230. *See also* conflicts
dream life, 6, 243. *See also* desired outcome

EEOC. *See* Equal Employment Opportunity Commission
elevator pitch, 85–86, 97
emails
   address and signature, 58–59
   alternatives to using, 54, 55–56
   BLUF, 60–61
   boundaries around after-hours, 171–72
   cold outreach, 79–80, 81, 83–84
   concise and efficient, 59–61
   five steps to better, 57–63
   follow-up, 64–65, 94
   job offer response, 199–200, 202–3
   message length for, 56
   to micromanaging boss, 214
   networking, 77–84, 95
   new job relationship building, 165, 167
   out-of-context networking, 95
   preinterview, 63–64
   recipient name used in, 66
   to recruiters or hiring managers, 82–84
   rejection, 67
   scripts, 63–68
   subject line clarity, 59
   tone set in, 61–63
   tools for finding people's, 74
   unprofessional, 17
emotional/change conversation, 33, 35, 37
emotional/connection conversation, 33, 35, 37
emotions
   communication styles triggering, 19–21, 39
   feedback and, 220–24
   negotiations and, 139
   in quitting job, 226–32, 239
   rejection emails and, 67
   with rude coworkers, 208–9
   sticky situations and evaluation of, 198, 208
empathy, 198, 205, 209
employment. *See also* job offers; new job

employment (*cont.*)
   email scripts for seeking, 63–68
   hidden job market for, 70–72
   online networking for seeking, 80–84
   options for making connections, 97–98
   as transactional agreement, 141, 157
empowerment, 242–43
ending strong, with speech, 28–29
Equal Employment Opportunity Commission (EEOC), 124, 125
ethics and morals, 197, 200, 207. *See also* sticky situations
expectations. *See also* boundaries
   burnout with unrealistic, 162–63
   lesson around assumptions and, 3
   Me Problem / You Problem, 31
   reality of job compared with, 1–3
   underpromise and overdeliver approach to, 168–70
   understanding and setting new job, 168–72
eye contact, 49–50

factual/change conversation, 33–34, 37
factual/connection conversation, 33, 34, 37
feedback
   from bosses, 172, 214, 215, 221–22
   about bosses to HR, 232, 238–40

   emotions around, 220–24
   factual/change conversation and, 34
   giving, 223–25
   for Me Problem / You Problem discernment, 31–32
   Oreo Method for, 223, 225
   request in new job, 172
Ferriss, Timothy, 135
filler words
   higher-quality, 41
   use of, 40–42
flexibility
   interviews and, 120, 131
   negotiating skills and, 151, 154
   salary, 120, 154, 155
follow-up
   emails, 64–65, 94
   in networking, 94
forward-facing language, 46–48
The 4-Hour Workweek (Ferriss), 135
The Four Agreements (Ruiz), 103
freelance
   boundaries and, 180–81
   written communication and, 55

Gandhi, Mahatma, 28
Give and Take (Grant), 73
Gladwell, Malcolm, 17
Glassdoor, 231–32
goals, 91–92
   advocating for self, 184
   assertive communication, 38–39
   conversation, clarity around, 32–37, 85–86
   elevator pitch, 85–86

interview questions about,
    112–13
new job sharing of, 172–73
gossip and drama, 174, 179–80,
    208, 230
Grant, Adam, 73
Grey Rock Method, 208

hand gestures, 50
hidden job market, 70–72
high-level professionals, 72–74
hiring managers. *See* recruiters
    and hiring managers
honesty, 39, 49
    interview approach to, 114–15,
        117, 118, 119
    negotiations and, 144–45
    quitting job and, 238–40
Human Resources (HR), 190
    coworkers flirting and, 210
    feedback about boss to, 232,
        238–40
    new job bait and switch
        and, 204
    quitting job and, 232, 238–39
    reporting inappropriate
        behaviour to, 49, 178, 210,
        217, 219
humor, 217–19
hypermasculine approach,
    11–12, 147

impressions, last, 226
Instagram
    interview research and, 105
    networking and, 79
interest, showing, 92–93

interview questions and,
    131–32
rude coworkers and, 209
internship, 1–3
interruptions
    from coworkers, 191–93
    feedback example regarding,
        223–24
interviews
    AI help with, 102
    anxiety and remedies, 99–103,
        109–10
    asking questions in, 131–33
    basic question types and
        answers in, 110–23
    behavioural questions and
        answers in, 125–28
    body language in, 108–9
    check-in email after, 65–66
    clothing for, 104–5
    company focus in, 106–7, 113
    discrimination and, 123–25
    failures discussed in, 126–27
    follow-up email for, 64–65
    former boss questions in,
        117–18, 127–28
    greatest strength and weakness
        questions in, 115–17
    honesty in, 114–15, 117, 118, 119
    illegal or inappropriate
        questions in, 123–25
    know you audience in, 146
    negotiation research prior to,
        141–46
    90/10 Rule in, 116–17, 121, 126
    outlier questions in, 131
    overselling self in, 1

interviews (*cont.*)
　past, present, future formula for, 111–12
　positive self-talk and, 102
　practice, 102, 105–6, 134
　preinterview email for, 63–64
　reason for leaving last job question in, 117–19
　résumé questions in, 112, 121–22
　salary questions in, 119–20, 136–37, 153–54
　selling self in, 1, 113–16, 128
　STAR approach to stories in, 126
　technical questions and answers in, 129–30
　tips for mastering, 103–10
　as two-way street, 131
introversion
　in-person networking and, 85
　networking and, 5, 75
　power in, 5

jargon
　case for, 13–16
　misunderstandings with, 13–14
　purposes of, 14–15
　on résumés, 16
　tips for learning, 15–16
job market
　hidden, 70–72
　researching, 141–44
job offers
　bait-and-switch situations and, 203–4
　dual, handling, 199–201
　emails in response to, 199–200, 202–3
　start date negotiations and, 201
　vacation plans and, 202–3

kindness
　boundary setting and, 177–78
　clarity relation to, 1, 39
　feedback and, 223–25
　negotiations and, 147–49
　networking and, 82
　saying 'no' with, 186–87
　to self, 242–43
Kishimi, Ichiro, 30–31
Koga, Fumitake, 30–31

last impressions, 226
laughter, 217–19
leaders, 147
　forward-facing language of, 47
　reach networking with, 72–74
leadership, interview questions about, 128
leverage, in negotiations, 142–45, 153–54
LinkedIn
　networking and, 74, 76, 77–78
　profile set up on, 76
　staying connected with coworkers on, 237–38
listening skills, 117
　active, 26–27, 133
　feedback example regarding, 223–24
　interest and curiosity role in, 92–93
　interviewing and, 128, 133

masculine approach, 11–12, 147
Mehrabian, Albert, 48
mentors, 8, 145, 174
  reach networking and, 72–74
Me Problem / You Problem
  discernment, 29–32, 213, 214, 235
messaging platforms
  message length relation to choice of, 56
  Slack, 54, 55, 56, 166
microaggressions, 217–20
micromanagement, 213–15
mindset
  confidence element of, 21–23
  importance of correct, 18–19
  self-awareness element of, 19–21
mirroring
  body language, 51–52
  energy, 92
  in negotiations, 153
  networking and, 92
  verbal, 52–53, 153
mirror neurons, 51–52
morals and ethics. *See* ethics and morals; sticky situations
movement, for anxiety relief, 101, 109

negative self-talk, 102
  confidence impacted by, 22–23
negotiations
  aggressive communication and, 147
  authenticity and, 148
  avoid overexplaining in, 149–50
  collaborative approach in, 151, 152
  discomfort and fear with, 135–37, 139, 140, 161
  dual job offers and, 200–201
  early career, 138–39
  emotional impact of, 139
  example of successful, 152–56
  fairness in, 150
  flexibility in, 151, 154
  know your audience in, 146
  leverage in, 142–45, 153–54
  new job start date, 201
  nonsalary compensation, 155, 159–60
  for raise, 144–45, 156–59
  with recruiters, 152–56
  red flags in, 140
  research findings on, 138–39, 140
  research prior to interviewing, 141–46
  rules for, 147–52
  salary, timing for, 120
  severance packages, 160
  tact in, 151
  warmth in, 147–49
  worst-case scenario in, 140
networking
  career success relation to, 69–70
  elevator pitch, 85–86, 97
  events, 72, 85, 90–94
  fear of, 69
  follow-up in, 94
  hidden job market and, 70–72
  in-context, 90–94
  in-person, 84–90

networking (*cont.*)
  as introvert, 5, 75
  kindness and, 82
  negotiation research and, 141–42
  new job in-office, 167–68
  online, 75–84
  out-of-context, 94–98
  peer, 74–75, 97–98
  quitting job and future, 227, 237–38
  reach, 72–74
  reciprocity principle in, 73, 80–81
neurodiverse people, 49
neurons
  mirror, 51–52
  negotiations and, 139
Never Split the Difference (Voss), 226
new job. *See also* job offers
  bait-and-switch situation with, 203–4
  boundaries and expectations with, 168–72
  documentation and, 166–67
  feedback request in, 172
  first day reality with, 1–2
  guide to first ninety days of, 164–73
  in-office networking, 167–68
  quitting old job before starting, 229–30
  relationship building in, 164–66
  search kept from current boss, 233
  start date negotiations, 201

Newton, Howard W., 162
New York City sanitation workers, 143
nonsalary compensation
  negotiations for, 155, 159–60
  salary flexibility relation to, 120, 154, 155
  severance packages and, 160
nonverbal language. *See* body language

Ogilvy, David, 92
online networking
  cold outreach in, 79–81, 83–84
  with recruiters and hiring managers, 81, 82–84
  warm outreach in, 76–79
open-ended questions, 44–45
opportunities, 69, 99
  for connection, 44–45
  network growth relation to, 71
  positivity aiding in, 47
Oreo Method, for feedback, 223, 225
Orwell, George, 54
overtalking, 28–29
overwhelm
  boundaries for avoiding, 163
  communicating about, 29–30, 31, 38, 212–13
  forward-facing language about, 48

PAGE (Place, Activity, Goals, Exit), 91–92

INDEX

parental leave policy, 216–17
passive-aggressive communication
  bosses and, 38, 216
  in conflicts, 37–38
  defining, 38
  examples of, 38, 39–40
  self-reflection about, 39
passive communication
  defining, 37–38
  examples, 38, 39–40
  people pleasing relation to, 37–38
  self-reflection about, 39
peer networking, 74–75
  out-of-context, 97–98
people pleasing, 5, 121
  conflicts and, 30–31
  emails and, 62
  new job boundary setting and, 170
  passive communication and, 37–38
perfectionism, 117
persona, 9–11
personality
  email sign-off fitting, 58–59
  in interview, 131
  softening strong, 40–41
phone calls, 57
phrasing swaps. *See* word and phrasing swaps
physical appearance, 103–5, 109–10. *See also* body language; clothing
Place, Activity, Goals, Exit (PAGE), 91–92

podcasts
  articulate speech learning from, 24
  for interview preparation, 102
  for learning jargon, 15–16
  networking and, 77
positive language
  negative language replaced by, 45–46
  for self-talk, 23, 102, 144
positivity
  for career success, 45, 102
  in interviews, 108
  in negotiations, 147
  smiling and impact on, 50–51
posture, 51, 109
practice, 53
  interview, 102, 105–6, 134
  power of, 242
  small talk, 89–90
pregnancy, communicating about, 216–17
proactivity, 46–48
professional communication. *See also specific topics*
  assertive communication as goal for, 38–39
  authenticity in, 9–13
  common questions about, 8
  human-to-human, 9
  mastering, 4–5
  observing, 4
promotions
  asking for, 189–91
  lack of advocating for self and, 183–85
  title change and, 190–91

promotions (*cont.*)
   visibility of accomplishments and, 193–94
psychology, 147
   Adlerian, 30–31
   of body language, 48

questions, in conversation
   microaggressions and, 218
   no-facing, 158
   open-ended instead of closed-ended, 44–45
   repeating, technique, 25–26
questions, in interviews
   asking, 131–33
   basic types and answers for, 110–23
   behavioural, 125–28
   illegal or inappropriate, 123–25
   outlier, 131
   technical, 129–30
quitting job
   authenticity in, 236–37
   bosses negative response to, 229–30, 235–36
   emotional responses to, 226–32, 239
   future considerations when, 226–27, 237–38, 240
   giving notice when, 229, 233–34
   guilt and, 228, 235–36
   meeting with boss for, 234–35
   mistakes to avoid in, 229–32
   order of operations for, 233–40
   references/letter of recommendations and, 231, 237–38
   resignation letter for, 237
   scripts for, 235, 236

raises
   negotiations for, 144–45, 156–59
   phrasing when asking for, 43–44
reciprocity principle, 73, 80–81
recording self, 25
   for filler words, 41–42
   for interview practice, 106
recruiters and hiring managers
   negotiation as collaboration with, 152
   negotiation example story with, 152–56
   online networking with, 81, 82–84
references/letter of recommendations, 231, 237–38
referrals, 71–72
reframing language. *See* word and phrasing swaps
rejection, response to, 67–68
relationship-building
   caution with boundaries and, 174–76, 179
   with coworkers, 164–65, 167–68
   in new job, 164–66
repeating/summarizing speech
   active listening by, 26–28
   questions and, 25–26
resignation. *See* quitting job
résumés, 102, 145
   gaps in, 121–22

interviewing and talking about, 112, 121–22
jargon on, 16
Roberts, Nora, 135
Rohn, Jim, 196
Roosevelt, Eleanor, 243
Roosevelt, Theodore, 177
Ruiz, Don Miguel, 103

salary. *See also* negotiations; raises
   avoiding personal reasons for increase in, 149–50
   early career negotiations and, 138–39
   flexibility relation to compensation packages, 120, 154, 155
   initial offer of, 140, 154
   interview questions about, 119–20, 136–37, 153–54
   renegotiations in current job, 144–45, 156–59
   researching job market and, 141–44
   transparency laws, 142
'sandwich' technique, 25–26
sanitation workers, leverage of, 143
self-awareness mindset, 19–21
self-criticism, 22–23, 243
self-esteem, lacking, 102–3
self-love, 103, 242–43
self-talk
   negative, 22–23, 102
   positive, 23, 102, 144, 242–43
selling, 54–55

The 7 Habits of Highly Effective People (Covey), 6
severance packages, 160
silence, 28–29, 106, 136
Slack, 54, 55, 56, 166
slow talkers, 20–21
small talk
   inappropriate interview, 124–25
   introversion and, 85
   tips for mastering, 87–90
smiling, 50–51
   microaggressions and, 218
   negotiations and, 148
social media. *See also* LinkedIn
   interview research and, 105
   networking using, 74, 79
softener words
   'and' instead of 'but' as, 43–44
   use of, 40–42
sorry, saying, 40–41
STAR (Situation, Task, Action, Result), 126
sticky situations
   basic steps to handling, 197–99
   with bosses, 196–97, 212–17
   with coworkers, 204–12
   empathy in, 198, 209
   example of, 196–97
   feedback approach and, 220–24
   job offer, 199–204
   microaggressions and, 217–20
   pregnancy communication and, 216–17
strategic communication
   boundaries and, 177
   chess metaphor for, 7–8
   for desired outcome, 6–7, 242

Stromback, Rich, 69
summarizing speech. *See* repeating/summarizing speech
swaps. *See* word and phrasing swaps

tact, 162
  in negotiations, 151
technical questions, in interviews, 129–30
termination, from job, 230–31
texting, 56
therapy, 103, 232
thoughts, 'sandwich' technique for, 25–26
trust
  honesty with clients and, 127
  micromanaging boss and, 213–14
  physical appearance relation to, 103–4
Tutu, Desmond, 183

uncomfortable conversations, 135–36
uncomfortable situations. *See* sticky situations

vacation, 38, 133
  job offer and planned, 202–3
Van Edwards, Vanessa, 50
verbal communication fails
  conversation style and, 37–40
  conversation type misunderstanding, 32–37
  Me Problem / You Problem discernment and, 29–32
  softeners and fillers overuse/underuse, 40–42
verbal mirroring, 52–53, 153
vocal communication, 48
Voss, Chris, 226

warmth, of character, 147–49
word and phrasing swaps
  'and' instead of 'but,' 43–44
  forward-facing replacing backward-facing language, 46–48
  open-ended instead of closed-ended questions, 44–45
  positive replacing negative language, 45–46
  'what' or 'how' instead of 'why,' 42–43
words, power of, 241–43
workload
  aggressive communication about, 38
  boundaries around, 162–63
  communicating clearly about, 29–31, 211–13
  coworkers absence and increase in, 210–12
  emotional/connection conversation about, 35
  micromanagement of, 213–15
  passive communication about, 38
workplace communication. *See* professional communication; *specific topics*
'workspeak,' 13

written communication. *See also* emails
   'Bottom Line Up Front' approach to, 60–61
   evolution of workplace, 54
   format choice for, 55–57
   grammar and spelling checks in, 57
   message length considerations, 56–57
   mistakes in, 55
   personal names use in, 57, 66
   phone call choice over, 57
   for reach networking, 74
   recipient name used in, 66
   spelling and grammar checks, 57
   for texting, 56

You Problem / Me Problem discernment, 29–32, 213, 214, 235